The New English Dandy

Alice Cicolini

With 261 illustrations, 100 in colour

Thames & Hudson

P. 2: Alexander McQueen, Autumn/Winter
04/05 collection.
Right: Basting on a Kilgour suit jacket.

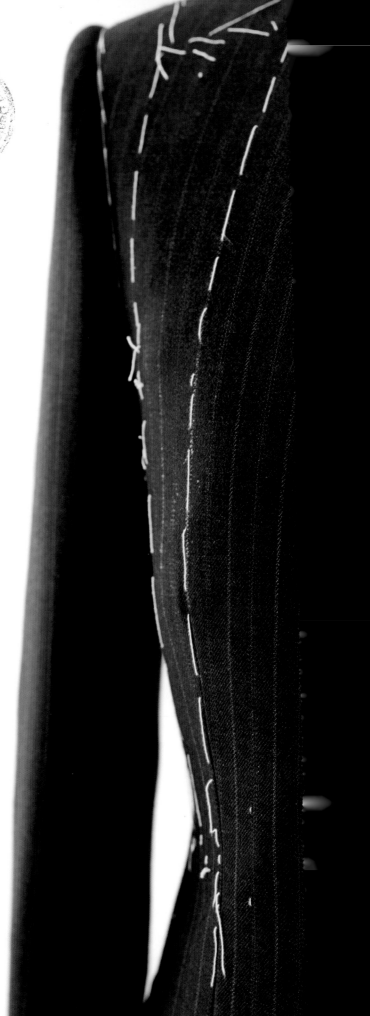

This book is dedicated to my parents, Leo and Liz Cicolini.

It is based on the British Council touring exhibition, '21st Century Dandy' that I developed throughout 2003. The original concept evolved through creative collaboration with five people: Dr Christopher Breward, Emily Campbell, head of design at the British Council, product designer Andrew Stafford, photographer Nigel Shafran and graphic designer Stephen Sorrell of Miles Murray Sorrell FUEL. As the UK's international cultural relations organization, the British Council was a particularly appropriate place in which to start to define such a markedly English concept.

For *The New English Dandy*, I would like to thank in particular Grace Woodward, for her sharp, perceptive selection and tenacious pursuit of sitters for the portraits, and all six photographers whose knowledge of and creative contribution to the subject have taken it in important and unique directions I could not have envisaged – Mark Blower, Antony Crook, Richard Dawson, Fiona Freund, Marius W Hansen and Philip Sinden.

Thanks also go to the designers, sitters, tailors and their teams for the energy and interest they have shown in the project. Notable contributions have come from Richard Anderson, Mat Bickley, Stephen Calloway, Damon Cleary, Siddhartha Das, Lucas Dietrich, Robin Dutt, Jason Evans, Simon Foxton, Simon Fraser, Matthew Glamorre, Tom Greatrex, Catherine Hall, Terry Haste, Sorrell Hershberg, Nigel Lawson, Fiona McEwen, James Main, Whitaker Malem, Alison Moloney, Non-Format, Gerrard O'Carroll, Alistair O'Neill, David Piper, Tom Price, Chris Sanderson, Stephen Sanderson and Paul Wright. Lastly, thanks to my husband and family of friends without whose support neither exhibition nor book would ever have been completed.

First published in the United Kingdom in 2005 by
Thames & Hudson Ltd, 181A High Holborn, London WC1V 7QX

www.thamesandhudson.com

British Library Cataloguing-in-Publication Data
A catalogue record for this book is available from the British Library

ISBN-13: 978-0-500-51268-5
ISBN-10: 0-500-51268-X

Printed and bound in Singapore by Star Standard Industries (Pte) Ltd.

Opposite: Quentin Mackay, 2002 collection
(see p. 9).

Foreword

In the spring of 2003 I spent many illuminating hours in the company of Alice Cicolini visiting the headquarters and retail outlets of traditional family firms, high-street multiples and independent designers whose products defined what we perceived to be a moment of 'renaissance' in the creative fortunes of the British menswear industry. The material we amassed provided the basis for the highly successful, prescient and innovative British Council touring exhibition '21st Century Dandy', the content of which has also informed the themes of this book, and I am extremely pleased to see our endeavours developed in this way. For while the literature on men and fashion is growing, it is in many ways a neglected subject with many social, aesthetic and cultural implications that deserve deeper scrutiny.

When we approached potential contributors to the exhibition with our ideas, the term 'dandy' became contentious, inviting an impossibly diverse range of interpretations and definitions. What seemed clear, though, was that since the glory days of Beau Brummell, the elite notion of dandyism as the rather shocking preserve of the gentleman had been undermined by the widening choices ushered in by the democratization of fashion in the twentieth century. Several commentators, nostalgic for the epochs of Count d'Orsay and Oscar Wilde, have seen this as a cause for regret. However, my sense is that a loosening up of things has had many positive effects, not least the ways in which a playful experimentation with issues of image and style can contribute to the breaking down of entrenched and divisive assumptions about identity. One of the key concepts of dandyism is the notion that seemingly frivolous statements betray a deep seriousness. In a related manner, the apparently superficial trappings of fashion culture can have far-reaching social and political effects. The stunning photography and provocative commentary that follow bear witness to the power of dandyism to do just this, to shift ideas about what it is to be a man in the midst of our media-saturated, body-obsessed, commodity-centred twenty-first-century culture. The richness of the response, both in terms of the quality of design and the mobilization of taste on display here, suggests to me that future historians of fashion will look back on our era with a sense of awe – as a time when the dandy came back into his own. Alice is to be congratulated for providing some stunning primary evidence.

Dr Christopher Breward
Victoria & Albert Museum, London, 2005

Introduction

Walking down Oxford Street is usually a salutary lesson in the state of mainstream English sartorial trends. For men, the last few decades have been awash with trainers, tracksuits and FCUK at one end and Giorgio Armani and Prada at the other. So, it was surprising to see, in the spring of 2001, a young man wearing a Savile Row suit, Jermyn Street shirt and handmade brogues turn the corner into Hanover Square. For a number of weeks following that first sighting it seemed that several similarly well-dressed men had begun to populate the streets of central London. Something, it seemed, was happening to the English male.

Some years prior to this, the sense that suits, rather than tracksuits, and clubs, rather than clubbing, were about to become *de rigeur* for the urban gentleman had been propagated by such magazines as *The Idler* (first published in 1993) and *The Chap* (issue 1 appearing on the newsstands in mid-1998). Both publications, despite their differing focus, urged a radical reinterpretation of contemporary life. A rejection of mass-marketed leisure and the drudgery of corporate work, their manifestos advocated the return of Saint Mondays (a sixteenth-century peasant custom of absenteeism and drinking), of gentlemanly courtesy, of poetry, prose and absinthe, of pipe smoking and masculine camaraderie – and of correctness in dress. *The Chap* in particular offered guidelines for aspiring 'chaps' on the fine art of suiting and accessories. The magazines' exhortations appeared to fall on responsive ears, as private gentlemen's clubs proliferated and, as

The Chap's editor Gustav Temple states, communities of chaps began to congregate across the country brought together by publications like his, 'lost souls pursuing the things the magazine is about'.

These chaps are not alone. The new millennium has brought a slow but steady emergence of a new, dapper man, converging with other, similarly strict and measured masculine trends across London and in other urban centres. This book reflects the surging international profile of British menswear and focuses on six styles that define the contemporary English dandy. 'The Gentleman' explores the inheritors of a classic tailoring elegance, masters of subtlety and detail; 'Neo-Modernist' illustrates the reappearance of Modernism in English style and its heritage; 'East End Flâneur' highlights a particular, bohemian dandy, informed by environment, music, art and design; 'Celebrity Tailor' presents the arbiters of superstar taste and notoriety; 'Terrace Casual' portrays the Mancunian revivalists of working-class style; and 'New Briton' showcases designers and dandies engaged in re-interpreting contemporary national identity.

Whilst there is a vast difference in the way this sartorial revolution is made manifest – the Springcourt trainers of the Mancunian Terrace Casual a world apart from the John Lobb brogue of the Marylebone Gentleman – there are shared traits underpinning the deliberate choices these men are making. Consideration, neatness, awareness of the importance of detail, appreciation of line, investment in quality

Right: Illustration of George Bryan 'Beau' Brummell by Robert Dighton (1805). Here, at the height of his fame, Brummell is wearing the clothes on which his name was made: white linen cravat, navy-blue worsted-wool tail coat, breeches and highly polished riding boots.

Far right and opposite, left and middle: Hazlitt's hotel and Rules and Adam Street restaurants. All three establishments play on the themes of quality, discretion and clubbish exclusivity that defined Brummell's time, although Rules is the only one at which Brummell may have eaten, having opened in 1798 and been a favourite of King Edward VII.

Opposite, far right: Burlington Arcade. In Brummell's time, the arcades were as much a forum for parade as they were sites of conspicuous consumption. This may be less true today, but arcades are still home to some of England's most traditional purveyors of luxury goods.

and an enjoyment of a certain distinction that an understanding of these elements combine to afford – all are characteristics that defined the style of the original dandy's dandy of 1790s Regency[1] London, George Bryan 'Beau' Brummell.

If there is one figure in whom all the contradictions of masculine dress style in England is epitomized, it is Brummell. He was, in essence, a flamboyant puritan; a man who rejected the trappings of a cosseted aristocratic lifestyle, the silks, velvets and lace cut to create an exaggerated figure, whilst at the same time displaying a shrewd recognition of the importance of aesthetics, form and line in the making of the modern man. His life was in many respects revolutionary: the son of an equerry in the court of George III, he rose to extraordinary fame in an era of significant social upheaval. His early military career provided access to aristocratic and courtly circles where he swiftly befriended the Prince Regent, an association – intended or otherwise – that was to affect a decade-long and radical change in courtly dress style and manners.

Brummell's name topped the announcements of society party lists, his pronouncements on anything from debutantes to coat-tails were eagerly awaited, his choice of tailor and glove-maker avidly recorded. He was both nucleus of and ringmaster for an era of studied languor and detachment, of discreet but pointed extravagance and distinction (he is said to have polished his boots with champagne). His dress, while sombre and restrained, was made of the finest materials, shaped by the best craftsmen London had to offer (many of them often working on one item – the fingers and the thumb of his gloves were made at separate establishments) and worn with acute attention to detail, grooming and dressing in search of perfection.

Essentially, there is little documentary evidence to suggest that Brummell was anything more than an ardent and informed consumer, acutely aware of the power that subtle and refined, rather than overt and brash, display could provide. Brummell lived in the heart of London's golden triangle bordered by St James's, Piccadilly and Regent Street; he frequented exclusive gentlemen's clubs; commissioned clothing and accessories and furnished his interiors from Bond Street and Savile Row; and indulged in a pampered and leisured lifestyle of races, nocturnal entertainment and idle witticisms. All were interests that required considerable financial resource, although in Brummell's case he is said to have paid in publicity generated rather than hard cash. Regency dandyism was, ultimately, a celebration of the material superiority of urban life, and in many ways Brummell had simply taken advantage of a shift in the focus of fashionability away from Paris, a result of the upheavals of the Revolution, to promote the possibilities of high-quality consumption that London had to offer. Literary critic Ellen Moers, in *The Dandy*, her 1960s exploration of dandyism from the late 1700s to the 1950s, stated:

Legend is confused about the nature of [Brummell's] style. The popular version has always been that he dressed too obviously well, with fantastic colours and frills, exotic jewels and perfumes. The accurate (and important) report declares that he dressed in a style more austere, manly and dignified than any before or since....Brummell established a mean of taste appropriate to this last Georgian age, which took pride in its application of the principles of restraint, naturalness and simplicity to the modest spheres of interior decoration and personal appearance.[2]

The idea of the dandy is one that has both fascinated and repelled the English for centuries since Brummell's demise. Moers's comment contains two important nuances that inform this ambiguous relationship with dandyism. The first, that records of the 'Beau' and his style are located firmly in the region of legend rather than fact; the second, that dedicated investment in appearance and surroundings is somehow a meek and unambitious pursuit for a gentleman.

Brummell was certainly mythologized by a number of writers, mainly French, who transformed his taste into a way of life. The literary definitions that appeared in Paris in the 1800s – Edward Bulwer-Lytton's *Pelham: Or, the Adventures of a Gentleman*, Jules Barbey D'Aurevilly's *Du Dandysme et de Georges Brummell* and Charles Baudelaire's *Le Peintre de la vie moderne* – positioned dandyism in an altogether different sphere. Bulwer-Lytton gave it maxims,[3] D'Aurevilly turned

diary recordings of Brummell's life into a handbook for an attitude and a lifestyle and Baudelaire remodelled the dandy as a modern hero, a political, spiritual and social revolutionary. Later on in the same century, Oxford scholar Walter Pater drew on Baudelaire's potent blend of idealized dandyism and the English Romantic to create his own manifesto of decadent aestheticism. Pater abhorred vulgarity and revered beauty, both of the self and one's surroundings, and his incitement to make of one's life a work of art was most famously realized by Oscar Wilde. The desire to challenge the status quo through the veneration of style and beauty unites later radical, bohemian and flamboyant dandyism from Wilde, through the Sitwells' intellectual elitism and the media manipulation of Andy Warhol, to the star theatrics of Mick Jagger and Jimi Hendrix, the glam rock of David Bowie and the performance art of Leigh Bowery – all, of course, now legends in their own right.

The literary juxtaposition of aestheticism against puritan morality is at the heart of contemporary perceptions of the dandy. D'Aurevilly suggested that:

Nowhere has the conflict between the dictates of convention, and the tedium they generate, made itself felt so strongly in its habits and customs as in England.... And it is perhaps from this running conflict...that the profound originality of this puritan society springs.[4]

Right: Poet and playwright Oscar Wilde (1882). The photograph shows Wilde as a young man at the height of his engagement with the Aesthetics movement. Later in life he renounced extravagant velvets, silks and lily buttonholes for a more sombre, tailored style.

Far right: '3 Nigerians' (c. 1970). Postwar immigrants into Britain from Africa and the Caribbean brought new, more flamboyant looks inspired by Brooks Brothers and Savile Row, which powered British street style in the decades that followed.

Opposite, left: Reading chairs designed by Andrew Stafford (2003). The chairs, designed for the British Council touring exhibition '21st Century Dandy', encapsulate the combined pastimes of leisure and intellectual pursuit in which many a dandy has indulged over the centuries.

It is a suggestion that has informed the use of dress, and in particular the practice of dandyism, as a form of political commentary. Whilst, when asked, many of the spruce men whose portraits appear in this book were originally uneasy with a definition of their dress style as 'dandy' (their understanding of the word informed by an effeminizing and oppositional interpretation), there were a corresponding number who actively positioned themselves as inheritors of a politicized lineage. Club and music promoter Matthew Glamorre (see opposite) is an archetypal dandy and agitator for whom the mythologizing of dandyism was undoubtedly part of the originators' intentions:

To me, dandyism is socio-political confrontationism through dress. True dandies satirize their times, leaders, public and politics. Dandyism is a refusal to play by society's rules of banality and conformity. Whether these rules are aesthetic, social or political, the dandy is a self-ostracized outsider. Great dandies are endlessly quotable; they understand self-promotion, that personality, appearance and reputation combined in the right amounts confer mythical status. They are true revolutionaries.

For all the fervent admiration the dandy has inspired in some quarters, it has also stimulated corresponding and vicious satire. Oscar Wilde's homosexuality served to confirm in many minds what the term 'dandy' had, to that point, merely implied.

Both British and French satirists played on the inherent effeminacy, as they saw it, of a man so totally invested in the 'modest sphere' of aesthetic appreciation. Most famous of these satires was English author Thomas Carlyle's *Sartor Resartus*, first published between November 1833 and August 1834 in *Fraser's*, a magazine deeply suspicious 'of foreign affectations and domestic degeneracy'.[5] *Sartor* was pointed in its criticism:

The dandy…is an inspired man (inspired with the all-importance of Clothes), a creative enthusiast (enthusiastic over clothes), a poet (of Cloth – 'in Macaronic verses'), a (Clothes –) prophet, and a (Clothes –) martyr.[6]

For Carlyle and his followers, dandyism's fascination for the material was an intellectual weakness, the dandy an empty shell devoid of character and meaning. Holding up a mirror of poverty and class hatred to the Regency's pampered body, the arguments put forward in *Fraser's* were powerful ones that have been endlessly deployed before and since Carlyle's time.

Fashion theorist Christopher Breward proposes in his essay 'The Dandy Laid Bare' that the satirical attacks on the dandy's 'faintly ridiculous persona'[7] that proliferated in the Regency period were symptomatic of society's unease when faced with modernity and the rise of consumer culture. Breward argues that:

Right: Mick Jagger performing with The Rolling Stones, Madison Square Gardens (26 June 1975). Jagger embodies the fertile relationship between fashion and music, his style a pivotal part of his performance of rebellious celebrity.

Far right: The Grace Brothers, Matthew Glamorre and Jim Warboy (2004). Glamorre is a club promoter, performer and producer in the style of such performance artists as Alfred Jarry and Leigh Bowery. He has single-handedly created a contemporary cultural space for the 'gloriously disaffected'.

In the hands of Parisian literati the rarefied practice of thinking about clothing ultimately succeeded in belittling any serious consideration of the trace of its...production and consumption, a phenomenon that would have amused a practical man of the wardrobe like Brummell.[8]

He suggests that, as much as the literature and satire conforms to the picture of dandyism as a 'mannered denial of sordid realities...through the deliberate manipulation of appearance', it also linked with:

popular debates and widely held concerns over the moral state of masculinity, the advances of consumerism and the temptations of city life that informed a more generalised understanding of male corporeal behaviour, fashionable display and sartorial desire at the turn of the century.[9]

It is no coincidence then that dandyism has emerged during periods of intense uncertainty in relation to masculine identity: the 1780s crisis of Regency aristocracy, the 1890s scandal surrounding Wilde's homosexuality, the 1950s postwar wave of immigration and rise of the teenager and the 1970s era of women's liberation and Stonewall.[10] Since 1980, Britain has witnessed the character of the male change with whirlwind speed – the New Man, followed swiftly by the *Loaded* Lad and most recently, in the early twenty-first century, the Metrosexual.

If journalist Nick Compton's 2004 essay for *i-D* magazine, 'Where now for the Straight Guy?', is anything to go by, the popular mythology of masculine consumption as the sole preserve of the deviant effeminate still holds significant sway. The new Metrosexual, Compton suggests, is the return of the 'gentleman "poof"...a glorious parade to mock traditional models of masculinity and mark their passing'.[11] His position, that this decline can only be replaced by effeminacy, is a conservative one. There was little in Brummellian dandyism, nor in gentlemanly behaviour, that had anything to do with homosexuality – more, theirs were middle-class, aspirational values. Compton's thesis, as with nineteenth-century satire, reveals 'more about the general relationship between men, their bodies and their clothes at this confusing time'[12] than it does about the dandy.

Perhaps the rise of the twenty-first-century dandy has more to do with self-actualized consumerism, with a society newly at ease with industrial modernity, than it does with any effeminization of traditional masculinity. As art finds its way into luxury goods and luxury goods find their way into art, there are signs that commodity culture is going in search of the elegance, spirituality and aestheticism typical of Regency dandyism. The steady blending of art and luxury that Brummell may well have recognized has been driven by twenty-first-century dandies like the ones featured in this book. Writes journalist and director of London's Institute of Contemporary Arts Ekow Eshun:

Young Creatives are the generation of 20 somethings to 30 somethings who have chosen to transmute their boredom and frustration with branding and celebrity culture into a search for their own means of expression.

Where international branded goods once offered opportunities for differentiation, their widespread accessibility and the global uniformity of the collections have devalued their potential for individualism and self-definition (something acknowledged, for example, by Comme des Garçons' designer Rei Kawakubo's decision to develop items specifically for certain markets, perpetuating a new kind of consumer tourism). Now, the energy that has built up around the desire to create a unique identity has driven consumers toward dress that either offers the opportunity to show their own hand in the process of creation (i.e., tailoring) or is available in such small quantity as to make it virtually inaccessible to anyone else (i.e., rare trainers, vintage clothes). Eshun goes on to quote the publisher of London lifestyle magazine *Good For Nothing*, Neil Boorman (see p. 76), who says:

People want to be inspired and provoked. It's clear that we're heading towards a sterile monoculture but there's no point moaning on about it. We need to rebuild a culture for ourselves.[13]

The culture that is being built is one of experience and appreciation, of personal expression and of engagement with modernity (travel, technology and urbanity), all qualities inherent in dandyism.

In addition, there are also signs that the finality implied in Boorman's 'sterile monoculture' is not yet fixed, and that the dandy preserve of appreciation of elegance and aesthetics is more widespread than we might believe. The huge commercial success, despite its ubiquity, of good, affordable design (Jonathan Ives's Apple iMac and iPod, Tord Boontje's Garland for Habitat, Philippe Starck's lemon squeezer for Alessi) and the rise in attendance figures for cultural events and institutions (over 200,000 people visited Tate Modern in one day to view the art of one man, Olafur Eliasson) suggest that the appreciation of 'content culture' is not as niche as it has been in the past. Victoria Postrel, quoted in brand forecasting bible *Viewpoint*, argues:

We are increasingly engaged in making our world special. More people in more aspects of life are drawing pleasure and meaning from the way their persons, places and things look and feel. Whenever we have the chance, we are adding sensory, emotional appeal to ordinary function.[14]

Former MP and writer George Walden in the introduction to *Who Is a Dandy?*, his recent translation of D'Aurevilly's treatise on Brummellian dandyism, echoes Postrel when he writes:

Our own obsession with style and fashion is...

developing in an age of unprecedented leisure, which now extends through much of society, and an aspiration towards elegance, if not elegance itself, has come within the reach of millions… Does the democratisation of dandyism imperil taste – Brummell's god of gods?[15]

Retailers like Stephen Sanderson and Nigel Lawson (see pp 128 and 121) of Oi Polloi in Manchester would argue to the contrary; Oi Polloi is hardly a mass-market chain, but their mission is to provide the best in functional, beautiful design to those who choose to look for it. It may be that we are witnessing less the death of traditional masculinities than the ascendance and democratization of a particular kind of masculinity that celebrates rather than demonizes the finer things in life. Christopher Breward rightly indicates that there are two kinds of dandyism:

One associated with [Wildean] political, sexual and social resistance, the other with a commercial and corporeal engagement with the urban marketplace – [they] require careful unravelling if the defining features of the latter are not to be subsumed by the polemics of the former.[16]

The New English Dandy attempts to successfully unravel the two by exploring the varied interpretations of dandyism laid out across the centuries and by making the case for the way in which these diverse understandings have informed contemporary masculine identity in twenty-first-century metropolitan England. There is little evidence to suggest that Brummell intended anything more than to be the ultimate 'clothes-wearing man';[17] this does not invalidate all the manifestations that followed, but may well help to explain the breadth of interpretation, provided by interviews with dandies and those who dress, photograph and write about them, contained within this book. As Matthew Glamorre suggests in his interview (see p. 70) 'contrariness is central to the dandy' – uniting these modern typologies, however, is what essayist and dandy Max Beerbohm identified in the 1950s as the 'art of costume'. 'Dandyism,' Beerbohm wrote, 'is ever the outcome of a carefully cultivated temperament, not part of the temperament itself.'[18]

The Gentleman

The standard-bearer for contemporary quality informed
by tradition, the epitome of sartorial propriety.

Right: H. Hunstman & Sons, Savile Row. Henry Huntsman established his West End business in 1849, before moving to 11 Savile Row in 1919. The company has come to stand for classic English tailoring.

Opposite, left: Renovated silk plush top hat and Monte Cristi classic panama by Lock & Co. The oldest family-run hatters in the world, Lock & Co. has been at its current address in St James's since 1676. Clients include such dandies as Brummell, Oscar Wilde and Cecil Beaton.

Opposite, right: Hunting belt by Bill Amberg. A Notting Hill institution, Amberg encapsulates the new aristocracy of taste that borrows from conservative tradition and contemporary styling. Amberg launched a range of products for shooting in 2003.

Brummell's direct stylistic descendant is The Gentleman. The concept of *gentillisme* or gentlemanly behaviour began in England following the Norman Conquest, when new hereditary laws introduced by William, Duke of Normandy saw property pass directly to the eldest son. Devoid of inheritance, younger sons sought employment elsewhere, which in England, unlike France, was fairly easy to come by. The consequent social mobility resulted in a need to establish distinction of another kind. The beauty of the term 'gentleman' was its ambiguity; easy to determine what it was not, the job of describing what it was, was infinitely more difficult. In France, *gentillisme* was related to nobility; in England, however, a gentleman came to represent morality, adherence to a code of conduct that could as easily be displayed by men of humble origins as those of wealth and status. Today, as in previous centuries, our understanding of what constitutes a gentleman remains elastic. The easy, natural association with property, rural and urban, is reflected in an apparent effortlessness of dress, manners and social standing.[1] In the twenty-first century, however, it is an aristocracy of talent rather than birth that The Gentleman represents. The new Gentleman's most important quality is success and the power that success affords; second, is the reflection of his power through discreet and coded means.

A Gentleman is not a showman of any kind. For Hugh Lowther, 5th Earl of Lonsdale, described by writer Philip Mason as 'almost an Emperor, but never quite a

gentleman',[2] ancient lineage was no protection for an image tarnished by extravagance and impulsion. Whilst Lowther's bright-yellow livery, sportsmanship and common touch won him admirers from around the world, they simultaneously distanced him from gentlemanly society. Newness, excessive displays of wealth and other forms of vulgarity (usually related to public rather than private behaviour) were an anathema to the gentleman. The Regency dandy's wit, self-contained elegance and general superiority were for display in restricted arenas. Equally, today's gentlemanly style avoids ostentation. Brummell's gentlemanly descendants favour the sartorial anonymity of monochrome; the muted elegance of a grey or navy suit, black lace-up shoe, white shirt and modestly colourful tie reflect the subtlety of Brummell's own approach.

This discretion is evident in both the style of The Gentleman's clothes and the way he buys them – in the privacy of the tailor's suite. Gentlemanly dress is loaded with expressive clues: the turn of a collar or cuff, the size and style of a button and the colour and fastening of a shoe let the world know what kind of person you are or wish to be. It is, however, less simple now than in the nineteenth century for these coded forms of communication to remain quite so hidden. As sociologist Elizabeth Wilson explains:

It is no longer possible unreflectively to be the perfectly dressed gentleman whose [clothing] never draws attention to itself; we have all become so sophisticated about

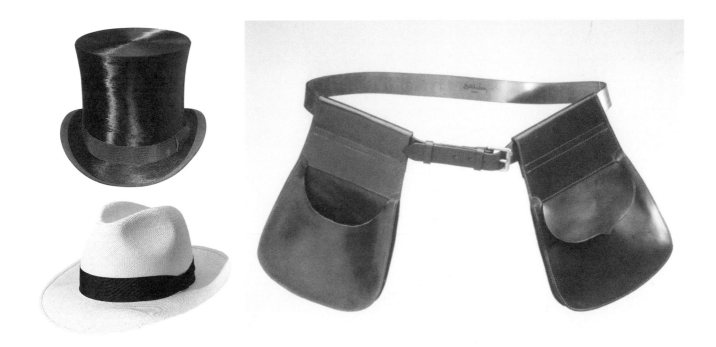

performance that we easily recognise the attempted sleight of hand that aim[s] to suggest the absence of effort.[3]

Contemporary tailors Timothy Everest, Charlie Allen, Carlo Brandelli and Richard Anderson are the drivers for gentlemanly discretion in the twenty-first century, Their studios are located in important centres of power and influence (Spitalfields, Islington and Savile Row), reflecting the status of many of their clients. Whilst they uphold key values – quality, propriety and discretion – these tailors bring a fresh eye to an established sartorial tradition.

Charlie Allen opened his first studio in 1982. The third generation in a family of tailors (his grandfather began his tailoring career in the Caribbean before emigrating to the UK), Allen studied menswear at the Royal College of Art, later going on to teach there for over two years in the early 1990s. Allen's signature style is weightless, stripped-down drape with a soft, natural shoulder line; 'it should look like it's made by an angel'.

Richard Anderson led the tailoring team at Huntsman before establishing his own label in 2001, specializing in a rakish line and experimentation with fabric. In the time since he opened, his client list has rapidly expanded beyond his wildest dreams. Anderson is clear that he is principally a tailor and aligns his success to the new generation of men concerned with their appearance and betterment:

Design is simple for a tailor with artistic flair. But a designer without thorough sewing training cannot tailor. There is a whole world of people who want to be wooed by innovation and novelty allied to quality and service. Today people want to be better (education), they want to be fitter (gym), and they want to look younger (spas or plastic surgery). I can make them look better and younger by making them clothes that not only fit them but suit their bodies and personalities.

Brandelli and Everest collaborate with some of the most important creative minds working in Britain (Nick Knight, Peter Saville and the graphic-design studio FUEL) to project their vision, whilst the studios of Anderson and Allen deploy the language (and content – both are collectors of modern art) of the contemporary art gallery to position their work firmly in what futurologist and editor of *Viewpoint* Martin Raymond describes as the 'New Luxury' generation. If it is no longer wholly possible to be a perfect Gentleman without showing some signs of deliberate consideration in dress, it is quite viable to live as one, as the passion for poetry, prose, theatre, art, design, good conversation and fine dining displayed by The Gentleman demonstrates.

Interview with Timothy Everest

Timothy Everest is one of the architects and leading practitioners of what he describes as the 'new bespoke

Right: Tommy Nutter in his Savile Row store (1 November 1969). Nutter is credited by many of the dandies and tailors in this book as an inspiration, mining as he did the rich seam of interpretation afforded by contemporary reworkings of classic style.

Opposite, left: Timothy Everest's 'house of clothing', Spitalfields. Everest has lovingly restored this exquisite Huguenot house. It is the perfect setting for his particular brand of immaculate, understated and contemporary Englishness.

Opposite, middle: Shooting muff by Bill Amberg. Amberg developed a range of shooting accessories because he had hunted from a young age. The vogue for traditional aristocratic sporting pursuits has ensured the range's success.

Opposite, right: Double monk-strap shoe by John Lobb. The original John Lobb made his name as a cobbler during the late-nineteenth century when he shod the feet of the Prince of Wales, later King Edward VII.

movement'. He opened his studio in the early 1990s after an apprenticeship with Tommy Nutter and has worked as a creative consultant to some of Britain's best-known brands, most recently, DAKS and Marks & Spencer.

AC: For you, what is the classic British tailoring style?
TE: Structured but slightly clumsy (obvious stitching is classically British bespoke), painstaking detail, a slight military feel and an eccentricity in the choice and matching of fabric.
AC: How would you describe what you set out to do with Timothy Everest, the characteristics of the house?
TE: I've always been interested in the history of British tailoring and have to admit to a degree of nostalgia, of looking at that history in quite a patriotic, rose-tinted-spectacles kind of way. So what I try to achieve with Everest is to take the essence of that quintessentially British style and to develop it into something more modern. I aim to communicate what I'm doing in a way that people today are more likely to understand – which is to propose bespoke as an alternative to luxury brands, and one over which the consumer has a significant degree of control. If I were to try and pinpoint how that manifests itself, I'd say the Everest style is slimmer, handmade and focuses on colour and pattern. I started out with a three-button jacket and narrow, 1950s-inspired Edwardian trouser, but I'm currently doing a more square-shouldered, lower-fastening one-button that draws the eye towards the top of the body, so I do try and evolve the

silhouette over time. But, the important thing is that, whilst I do have a 'fashion' customer who might come to me for the Everest look, bespoke is really about giving the customer the choice and the control. It's helping clients to look their best.
AC: In your early career you worked for one of the Row's most famous figures, Tommy Nutter. How has this influenced the house style, if at all?
TE: He was a huge influence on me. I started my career at Hepworths, which was an old-fashioned gentlemen's retailer. Tommy, on the other hand, was the Formula 1 of Savile Row; he totally understood his craft, but also how to articulate it to a new and different audience. I was at Nutter's at the same time as John Galliano and I think three things – the sensibilities of a gentlemen's outfitter, an awareness of impeccable craftsmanship and the deliberate, designed flamboyance of Tommy and the Central St Martins style in which Galliano was trained – have had a considerable effect on my work. What I learned at Nutter's was the workings of a business and the aesthetics of 'good/bad' taste, of things that work even though ostensibly they shouldn't. I hold onto this image of the international Gentleman who buys his clothes on his travels around the world and matches his Savile Row suit with red silk socks bought in Spain; his style is off, but nonetheless beautiful.
AC: We've previously discussed the Britishness in Timothy Everest as a sort of Martin Parr-esque loving humour. How do you feel this manifests itself?
TE: At the moment we're producing our ready-to-wear

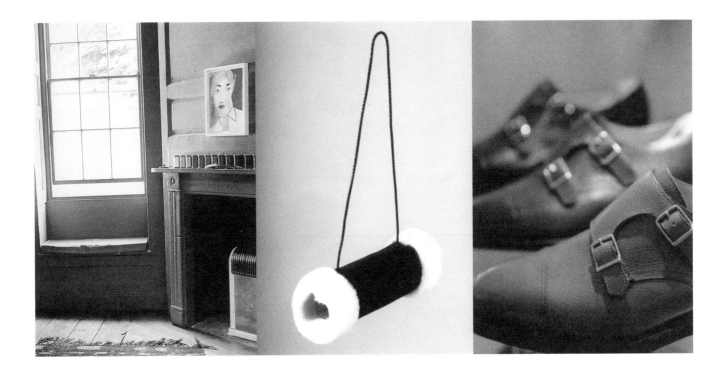

label, and that sense of humour is an intrinsic part of how the brand is developing. I think we've had to be quite careful about how it manifests itself though, because it would be easy to slip into a kiss-me-quick, down-by-the-seaside sort of approach, which frankly no-one can do with as much sophistication as Paul Smith. What we're looking at is how bespoke can translate to ready-to-wear, principally the addition of hidden details that you only discover after you've bought a piece and taken it home. It's taken me some time to understand where the British fit in and how we are perceived internationally; in essence, it's as the eccentric English gentleman, perfect shops, fog and high tea. It's important to hold on to what it is about these perceptions that is so attractive to people, whilst stripping out the dusty, boring, preserved-in-aspic feel of traditional England.

AC: You specifically chose a studio in the heart of Huguenot Spitalfields rather than the Row. Why?
TE: I'd like to say it was because I had a sixth sense about the area taking off, but really it was a romantic choice. I wanted a house of clothing and this is an incredibly beautiful one. I also didn't want to go to the Row because it would have felt like moving in with my parents and I wanted to be judged on the quality of what I did, not on the address. Ironically, a lot of the tailoring work commissioned on the Row that wasn't made in the West End was traditionally sent out to east London — we tend to send ours in the opposite direction.
AC: Arguably in a globalized marketplace for clothing,

bespoke is a very non-conformist route to take stylistically. Would you agree?
TE: Richard Jobson [post-punk rocker with the Skids, performance poet and film-maker] was one of my first clients and said to me that the double-breasted pinstripe suit was the new punk rock, almost as if wearing something so straight had become quite ironic, which was definitely a non-conformist view. It's a little bit more than that for me. It's certainly true that there is a real need for individuality, a movement towards the custom-made, and bespoke sits well in that context, but I actually dearly want tailoring to be normal. We all need choices and points of difference.

Interview with Carlo Brandelli

Carlo Brandelli is creative director of Kilgour. The son of an Italian clothing retailer, Brandelli made his name in 1993 with the opening of the modernist men's outfitter Squire on Cork Street, London.

AC: How would you define classic British tailoring and what is Kilgour's approach to that style?
CB: Kilgour exemplifies it: elegant, dignified, restrained, understated, fitted, proportionally correct and balanced. Stylistically, it's a narrow shoulder, slightly waisted jacket, clean chest definition and a flat-fronted, moderately narrow-legged trouser. We set out to be the definitive bespoke tailor and the first

Fitting room at Kilgour, Savile Row. The 2004 refurbishment of Kilgour's Savile Row store was driven by creative director Carlo Brandelli. A reviewer suggested that, without the clothing, the interior would work just as well as an art gallery.

truly modern, elegant luxury menswear brand to combine heritage and the finest craftsmen with modern, relevant design principles.

AC: How does Kilgour differ from the more traditional Savile Row cuts and fabrics?

CB: Firstly, it's about being open to design and relevant to the times in which we live. There's an element of costume drama about the Row, when actually people need visual change and stimulus. The only thing people don't want to change is the quality of the work, which we haven't for about one hundred years.

AC: How would you describe your client base and why do you think they choose Kilgour over other houses?

CB: The client base is joined by a common thread: they are informed about design and style and understand a man's wardrobe and what should be in it. Kilgour has a flare of cut and an understanding of style that only comes from years of making the finest clothes for some of the world's most demanding and celebrated clients. Everyone from Fred Astaire to Jude Law to Noel Gallagher has worn Kilgour – royalty, rockers and regiments.

AC: How does dandyism apply to your work and clients?

CB: A true dandy is what I'd define as a Gentleman, a man who understands the importance of wearing the correct thing, but is not obsessed with it. A Gentleman is confident and understands occasion, be it a formal state affair or a walk in the park.

AC: What defines gentlemanly dressing?

CB: A Gentleman is someone who knows about life and has perspective. I think the twenty-first-century

equivalent is simply a well-dressed man, a man who is comfortable and understands what he's doing sartorially. He can 'do' many styles – he knows which tailor to see for his charcoal grey, one-button, single-breasted suit, he knows which jean brand to be seen in, he understands which simple classic in the correct colour or shade is appropriate for a particular time. It really is an instinct.

AC: What, to you, are the key tailoring pieces for a Gentleman's wardrobe?

CB: A one-button, single-breasted, charcoal, Super 100–weight worsted-wool bespoke suit is the 'little black dress' of menswear. A navy, self-stripe, modern take on a blazer, worn with jeans, is a staple, as is a three-quarter-length covert coat in a charcoal-grey wool and cashmere mix. I'd include a puppy-tooth worsted-wool, single-breasted suit with a peak lapel for that über-cool event, and a single-breasted suit with slanted pockets in dark navy mohair with a slight two-tone. The one-button, single-breasted, chocolate brown suede jacket has also infiltrated the style circles of the twenty-first century.

Interview with Gustav Temple

Gustav Temple (see p. 39) is one of the founding editors of *The Chap* magazine, which, along with *The Idler*, has defined the new Gentleman movement.

AC: What do you understand dandyism to be?

Interior of Les Trois Garçons restaurant, Shoreditch, London. Launched by a trio of antique dealers, the restaurant showcases unique pieces from their collection of the fabulous and fantastical. Les Trois Garçons is a perfect example of updated gentlemanly style.

GT: A life dedicated to elegance and beauty and making a statement through clothing and attitude.

AC: Is 'chappism' the same thing as dandyism?

GT: Not quite, no. Dandyism is essentially interpreted now as superficial, which is part of its contemporary charm, whereas chappism is not – it's poetry, politics, a bit more about counterculture. Its mission is to reclaim a 1940s or 1950s version of Englishness and turn it into something radical. We're radicalizing the Gentleman. A Gentleman is witty, debonair and charming in everything he does, whether in conflict or in love. Gentlemen don't come from particular backgrounds; you might expect to find Gentlemen among the aristocracy, but you actually find them in lower echelons. A Gentleman must be one from the heart.

AC: Would you say you were a dandy, a chap or a Gentleman?

GT: I would say a chap above all, in the sense that a chap is a new concept, borrowing heavily from dandies and Gentlemen but hopefully creating something new. I'd say a major part of the chap's lifestyle is working in one's own time, not in an office, and not removing one's dressing gown until at least noon. Yesterday I was writing, doing interviews, taking tea with David Piper at the New Piccadilly Café, one of the last 1950s cafés in London. I bumped into other chaps there, discussed the new club I've opened, called the Sheraton Club, then headed off to the French House in Soho for a G&T. An ideal day would be a visit to the racetrack, cocktails at five around St James's and then a casino. This may

sound blazé, given that times are hard for all of us, but there's something of the bohemian in a chap, being dignified in penury, spending one's last fiver on a cocktail instead of in Sainsbury's.

AC: Have you always been a chap?

GT: I've always been interested in nice clothes, poetry, cutting a dash and have always been a fan of Oscar Wilde, Charles Baudelaire, P.G. Wodehouse – writers who have emphasized elegance. In my youth I succumbed more to the temptation of fashion; I was young in an age (the 1980s) when it was difficult to latch onto anything. Only on reaching middle age did I look for a stronger identity to see me through the latter part of my life.

AC: How important is the lifestyle and philosophy to dandyism, and chappism by extension?

GT: Very important. It's not about posturing, it's a whole way of life, an alternative existence in not such a different way to the punks and hippies. It's not accepting the status quo, not accepting that you should live the same way as others. I think dandyism and chappism are necessarily English philosophies since we have such a strong tradition of cult and subcultural movements. I suppose it boils down to an English eccentricity that I have felt lacking recently; there aren't quite as many eccentrics as there used to be, which might be why they are being celebrated again.

AC: What is it about the dandy that attracted you and led you to define the chap?

GT: I had always been a writer searching for the right

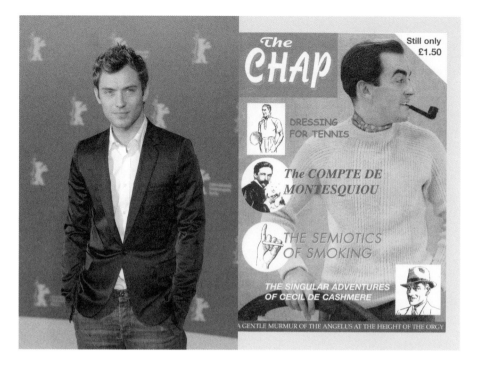

Right: Jude Law, 54th Berlin Film Festival (11 February 2004). Law is often cited as exuding a raffish twenty-first-century English style.

Far right: *The Chap*, cover of the first issue (1998). The magazine acts as a platform for views on sartorial correctness and gentlemanly lifestyle.

Opposite: Carlo Brandelli, creative director of Kilgour, in the store, Savile Row.

medium. I was writing broadsheet journalism, but found that I wanted to put my ideas into a magazine that was more like a manifesto, a way of grouping together people with similar ideas and aims. *The Chap* is a platform for sharing views and meeting others with similar views. I am realizing now that it's more than a media thing, it's also social and I find myself meeting chaps more regularly than I had before, attending other clubs, societies and events that are very chappist in themselves. *The Chap* is not didactic in the slightest, but it has, just by existing, brought together lost souls who were already pursuing the things *The Chap* is concerned with. It's more about defining interests than making lists – it's not a Sloane Ranger's handbook. To try and explain it too much would spoil it, but it is about individuality, and those who have come to it are mostly interested in the English look. The cultural identity of being English is so confused and forgotten, there's such a general embarrassment about Englishness, old-fashioned Englishness, among the masses, that there are people who have reached a point where they don't want to jettison tweed coats, black Labradors and so on.

AC: Is it really possible to be a Gentleman or a dandy today, to live the lifestyle and philosophy?

GT: One can believe in oneself as a Gentleman, live the life and so on, but it's not possible to be a Gentleman socially in that it's not widely appreciated or well received. To be a true Gentleman, there need to be ladies and gents who appreciate it. For so many chaps it's a question of maintaining perfect civility and politeness in the face of regular aggression and violence, of unsolicited ridicule. Having said that, only yesterday I went into town wearing a nice suit, hat and cravat, and this young man said 'you look good', but I suspect it's early days if a change in appreciation is to manifest itself. People are like pressure cookers and can't take the same thing for too long; the masses have been dominated by streetwear for a decade, and there's always a reaction when things get too bland. As for dandyism being equally difficult, I suspect it is, except people are so scruffy that in a strange way it's somehow *easier* than it might have been in Brummell's day. Put on a hat, carry a cane and, *voilà*, one's cutting a dash.

AC: What would Brummell be wearing today?

An elegant suit from Savile Row with a modernist twist, like a four-button jacket, that no-one would notice apart from tailors and other dandies. Maybe an eighteenth-century ring or snuff box. He would not have adopted one particular period – dandies and chaps I know wear clothes from the *fin de siècle* to the 1970s. Dandyism and chappism are basically about personal interpretation, having the range to express oneself. Formal clothing now is far less conservative than the fashions of young people, who all desire to dress the same and look like replicas of each other. They're meant to be the ones shocking us and yet here we are, the ones causing the sensation.

Opposite: Peter York, writer, at home,
Montagu Square, London.
Below: Peter York's tie (detail).

Page 28: Simon Thorogood, fashion designer,
at work, Victoria & Albert Museum.
Page 29: Tony Lutwyche, tailor, in his studio,
Berwick Street, London.

Opposite: Nick Foulkes, writer, at home,
west London.
Below: Nick Foulkes's sock and shoe (detail).

Opposite: Gustav Temple, editor of *The Chap*,
in Skinners Hall, Dowgate Hill, London.
Below: Gustav Temple's cravat and cuff
links (detail).

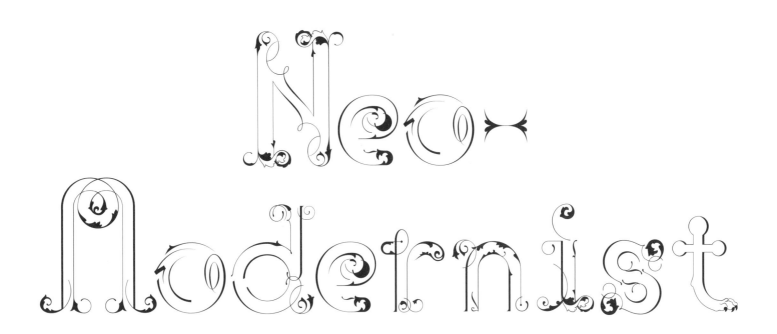

Neo-Modernist

Sharp tailored suits, with crisp, clean lines, cut from luxurious materials
in sombre tones, this wardrobe subverts tradition.

The twenty-first-century Neo-Modernist is defined by his ability to look backwards and forwards, to the street and the salon. Neo-Modernists are internationalist rather than nationalist, 'citizens of the world' united by a passion for music that has consistently defined Modernists' pared-down, razor-sharp style in the past. In the late-eighteenth century, it was the modernity of Beau Brummell's monochromatic tailoring that marked him out against the Baroque costume more commonly preferred by the English aristocracy. A 'figure in black and white',[1] his style was a rejection of frippery, the lavish texture, colour and surface detail favoured by his peers. In 1846, thirty years after Brummell's decline, French poet and modernist Charles Baudelaire wrote in *Le Peintre de la vie moderne*:

For the perfect dandy...enamoured as he is above all of distinction, perfection in dress consists in absolute simplicity, which is, indeed, the best way of being distinguished.[2]

The nineteenth-century definition of modernity was beauty inspired by an increasingly industrialized and urban context and a refusal of ancient ideals of the exquisite. For Baudelaire, the black suit, such a marked departure for aristocratic masculine dress, was an abstract reflection of contemporary society, typifying modernity as much as it was a fashion. The dandies who popularized it became, to him, modern heroes.

Almost a century later, modernity found new expression in Bauhaus architectural Modernism. Le Corbusier, a chief proponent of the Modern style, believed that 'ornament always [hid] some fault of construction'[3] and placed far greater emphasis on the use of contemporary technologies and the 'higher order' of structure and function. In twentieth-century England, Modernism struggled to communicate itself as a positive design choice, but there were periods of fervent engagement with its clean lines and sober formalism. In dress, these moments have, for the most part, stemmed from the emergence of the teenager, both in Britain and across the Atlantic in East Coast America, where in the 1940s modernity blended with youth culture. American zoot-suited hipsters, epitomized by swing exponent Cab Calloway, set the sartorial tone for teenage rebellion across the Western world. The Zooties 'challenged [the notion]...that dignity and a resplendent, stylish appearance are incompatible elements of masculinity,'[4] and the reverberations were felt as far away as France (with the appearance of the *Zazou*).[5] Later in the same decade, the East Coast Modernists – inspired by Gil Evans and Miles Davis's Modern Jazz Quartet, who recorded *Birth of Cool* (1949–50) on the cusp of a transformation in contemporary Western social history – turned down both the musical and sartorial temperature, setting out the rules for the following decade of 'cool'. They favoured a pared-down look, modern, sharp, slim and fitted, a look that stylistically mirrored their music.

The look was given a European twist by the mid-1950s Italian *pavoneggiarsi* (literally translated as 'to strut about', and derived from the Italian for peacock), encapsulated in *La Dolce Vita* (Federico Fellini, 1960), but it was the early-1950s British Mods who 'transformed this style into a religion'.[6]

In 1959, Colin MacInnes wrote *Absolute Beginners*, a prophetic assessment of generational divide that marked a more aggressive definition of teenage youth culture as it was emerging in England. In the character The Dean, MacInnes provided a template description of the early Mod:

college-boy smooth cropped hair with a burned-in parting, neat white Italian rounded-collar shirt, short Roman jacket very tailored (two little vents, three buttons), no-turn-up narrow trousers with 17-inch bottoms absolute maximum, pointed-toe shoes, and a white mac folded at his side.[7]

Greater financial independence and increased leisure time contributed to the development of subcultural style during this period. Early Mods were the first generation of working-class English youth who had grown up around West Indians and their look drew heavily on the personal innovation and creativity rooted in 1950s Caribbean style, which in turn had absorbed influences from Savile Row, Hollywood and the East Coast Modernists. These working-class dandies subverted conservative, mainstream dress

and attitude – suits, polished shoes, neatness, cleanliness – 'to create a style, which while being overtly close to the straight world was nonetheless incomprehensible to it'.[8] The Mod signalled his isolation from middle-class England through his choice of leisure pursuits, aligning himself with other marginalized groups and drawing on international urban culture, favouring American burger bars, jazz and R&B, Italian cafés and scooters, French clubs, films and haircuts. Dying out in the late 1960s, Mod culture was later resurrected in the 1970s, first by the group The Small Faces and later Paul Weller's The Jam. It remained international in its perspective, overlaying a more graphic, Op Art–inspired feel on top of the slim-fitted silhouette of its forebears.

In twenty-first-century England, clean lines and muted colours once more afford relief from the riot and parody of Postmodernism that has dominated British fashion since Vivienne Westwood and John Galliano. The Neo-Modernist style blends the major concerns of each modernist movement: contemporary abstraction, a focus on structure and materials and an internationalist outlook. It draws, as it did in Brummell's day, on established sartorial traditions, subverting them through materials (denim for suits, shirting fabrics for linings), form (tighter, sharper, leaner than the norm) and function. The contemporary monochrome suit might be made from utility fabric with structural details that would withstand physical labour, but it is in fact a costume for an urbane,

Right: Alexander McQueen, Autumn/Winter 04/05 (right) and Spring/Summer 2005 (far right) collections. McQueen, who started out as an apprentice on Savile Row, is one of the UK's foremost modernist fashion designers, focusing on structure, the architecture of clothing and the body.

Opposite, left: Union Jack Oxford shoe by Jeffery West. The national flag became a graphic emblem for the second generation of Mod culture, inspired by Pete Townsend and The Jam.

Opposite, middle and right: You Must Create (YMC), Spring/Summer 2005 collection. Fraser Moss, YMC's designer, draws on his personal style, inspired by early Mod culture, to produce the collections.

creative society at leisure in the cafés and smoky bars of Soho and Mayfair.[9]

The blend of Savile Row tailoring traditions with a Modernist perspective is epitomized by Alexander McQueen. In 2002, McQueen joined with Huntsman, one of the Row's most established bespoke houses, to create a capsule collection redolent with Modernist influence, from a take on the zoot suit to an extreme, lean version of Huntsman's traditional one-button silhouette. In early 2004, McQueen launched his own menswear collection, which he defines as ready-to-wear at Savile Row standard:

The construction and architecture of the pieces employ the core techniques I learned during my four-year apprenticeship on the Row. You have to fully understand the construction of clothes before you can begin to manipulate them. What I've done is to take these traditional techniques and inject modernity.

McQueen uses subdued colours in luxurious fabrics, allowing the details – velvet collars, gold-and-black bullion embroidery, fox-fur-trimmed hoods and grosgrain ribbon inside jackets and coats in either black or Mod-inspired red, white and blue – to signal allegiance to a subcultural style. The collection draws on inspiration as varied as:

Sombre morning suits and Jewish ceremonial dress, Mod and Skinhead crombies and blazers, slim-legged Mod trousers and one-button jackets, and 1970s romantic rock'n'roll. What I want to achieve is clothing for individuals, a focus on quality over trend.[10]

The club plays as important a role for the Neo-Modernist as it did for his forebears. Based at the Great Eastern Hotel in London's Liverpool Street, the Modern Times Club was launched in 2003. David Piper (see p. 55), and his business partner Johnny Vercoutre (see p. 75), opened Modern Times soon after the success of the Whoopee Club with which they were also involved. Both ventures have marked a revival of vaudeville performance as preferred entertainment for a generation dismayed by the 'general vulgarity and horribleness of going out, the lack of anything with genuine depth and interest'. Lifestyle is particularly crucial to Piper's interpretation of dandyism: 'anyone can wear a nice suit, it just sets you off as a well-dressed man'. It becomes acutely relevant, Piper feels, for a generation so used to reading visual images, 'when dandyism's coded sartorial subtlety is no longer possible'. Urban context is of defining importance to Piper:

I lived in Marylebone for a long time, mainly because I could walk. It makes such a difference to your life since living in a city can be quite brutal and walking is about the nicest way to experience it. As to the rest, I go to and run mid-week Soho clubs; I write a lot as a journalist, I've found I have the talent and charisma

for that; and I constantly develop new work, like *Wyndham's Wandering Woo-Woo Wagon that I took to the 2005 Edinburgh Festival. It's a one-person peep show in a Bajaj rickshaw, which is intended to convey a sense of Victorian backstreet entertainment.*

The theatricality of his work feeds into the clothes that he wears. Piper dresses from specific periods between 1890 and the early 1960s:

It's the quality of the clothes, the cars, the slowness of life, the glamour and theatricality of these periods that appeal to me, but it's in the mix of periods that you find the modernity. The excitement of modern life is about not adhering to old rules, about finding new things and being slightly naughty within a restrictive context. I certainly see myself as a modernist. We thought about the name of the club for a long time, and it seemed to us that modernity, finding the beauty in urban society, was about both looking back and looking forward.

Fraser Moss (see p. 57), designer for You Must Create, draws his inspiration from the post-1950s and the emergence of the teenager, of which the Mod is a part. Teds, Mods, 1950s American teen-gangs, Beatnik, 1950s Edwardian dandyism, Ska, 1970s two-tone and the Hard Mod (or Skin) all play a stylistic role in the development of his personal look and that of his brand, which he considers as a postmodernist label, 'clean cut and sharp'. Moss attributes the rise of the dandy to a rejection of corporate fashion and a desire to find individualism again:

Personally, dandyism is incredibly relevant to the way I dress. Since I design for myself, YMC is inflected with a dandy approach on many levels – it's a maverick style. Modernism was about always looking forward, although now it's misunderstood, interpreted in a retro way. For me, to be modern, to move forward, you have to look into the past to make something new.

The British attitude towards dress – which Moss defines as 'twisted humour' – is crucial to an understanding of his work:

Vivienne Westwood and Malcolm McLaren were an important influence. They were subversive, but within the boundaries of what you would wear. Maybe it's because the British are so uptight that we always have something to rebel against.

The seminal partnership between Westwood and McLaren is also the epitome of another pivotal factor in British style – the relationship between music and fashion. 'British pioneers in dress have always connected a look and a sound. The tribalism of music and fashion have been linked throughout my life.' Moss is an avid collector of vinyl, picking up records from around the world, particularly Italy. Graphics, many of

Right: Burro, Spring/Summer 2002 collection. Launched in 1990, Burro blends Op Art graphics reminiscent of the second Mod movement with technical, performance textiles.

Opposite, left: Leather driving gloves by Dunhill. Dunhill's history is rooted in the early days of motoring. Mobility, in the sense of travel, global outlook and upward mobility between the classes, was crucial to the sensibility of the Mods.

Opposite, middle: Interior of Spencer Hart, designed by Ou Baholyodin (2001). Nick Hart, founder designer of Spencer Hart, is a huge fan of Cab Calloway and the Modern Jazz Quartet, and Spencer Hart owes a debt to the time's sharp-suited aura of 'cool'.

Opposite, right: Two-tone Chelsea boot by Jeffery West. Guy West, founder designer of the brand (see p. 53), has melded two-tone, a standard of the jazz scene, with the Chelsea boot.

which are drawn from the late-1950s and early-1960s Italian Op Art sleeves in his collection, are prevalent in YMC collections, and the company name is based on a quote by graphic artist and American pioneer of industrial design Raymond Loewy: 'You Must Create your own design style'.

It was graphics, Italia 1990 World Cup T-shirts with the 'No Alla Violenza' (No to Violence) slogan, which launched the Burro label in 1990 (see p. 58). Olaf Parker and Susan Denney, design directors of Burro, are inspired by the DIY culture of the late 1970s and early 1980s, 'the idea that anyone could try anything and that glamour had nothing to do with social status, celebrity or money'. Although they see the 'strict rules and restrictive hierarchy' of Mod culture as a 'negative creative force', it is the Mod's dedication to dressing up and making an effort that interests them:

The development of an individual style, and subtle (and sometimes less than subtle) non-conformity is exactly what we're about. We have no manifesto beyond self-expression and creativity, although we have a very English approach to our work and indeed 'Englishness' is the thread that binds all our collections.

Soho tailor Tom Baker (see p. 51) describes himself as 'an Italian trapped in an Englishman's body'. From an early age, he was raiding his Italian mother's sewing box, taking apart jeans, darning things, buying fabric, customizing jackets with old buttons and wearing homemade cravats:

Dandyism is something I've always been interested in. I was particularly inspired by the John Leech cartoons of Les Incroyables, *dandies in cravats, very fitted suits, pointed shoes and high collars. When I was at university in Manchester loads of people used to tell me I looked like a bit of a dandy. I think creative people always feed off public comment, and it just certified what I was already thinking.*

Baker describes his style as 'street tailoring' based on Savile Row traditions, 'specific and specialized, but subversive and free'. The positioning of the pockets, top-stitching, optical illusions, box pleats and patches inside the jackets combine to produce garments that are a fusion of the English look – genuine bespoke, based on the Savile Row block – and an 'abused and punked-up' feel – based more on a Mod and glam-rock music heritage:

My work hits a lot of sub-cultural buttons from when Mod was prevalent. Personally, my look is extremely fitted, narrow and tight. It's actually an incredibly flamboyant style, because it's so difficult to achieve technically. It's really an artform and for me tailoring and art are intrinsically linked. You have to make a work of art for people to wear.

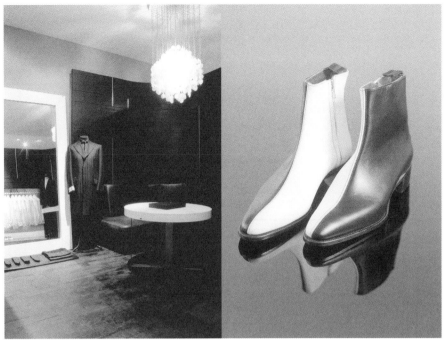

Interview with Nick Hart

When he launched Spencer Hart, Nick Hart (see p. 52) set out to offer 'clothing to get into trouble in'. Hart cites Noel Coward, the Duke of Windsor, Elvis Presley and Studio 54 as his principal influences, along with 1930s Hollywood and the 1940s American Be-Bop scene driven by Charlie Parker, Thelonious Monk and Dizzy Gillespie. The dominant inspiration, however, is Cab Calloway and the late 1940s East Coast jazz movement, 'I'm drawn to the old-school influence, the values of going out on the town, looking sharp, rewriting the rules within a narrow set of parameters'. Hart employs a monotone colour palette, cuts denim as deftly as worsted wool and works closely with British textile mills, often researching their archives for fabric references ranging from the 1930s to the 1950s. He is constantly refining his perfect white shirt and tailoring jeans as fitted and as sharp as his suits, which are defined by their elegant lines and narrow collars and are twinned with razor-sharp ties. Every suit is lined with black or white shirting cotton. Hart is nothing if not obsessed with detail. The store is a modern take on Savile Row's air of intrigue, of clubbish mystery, but it is one that references smoky jazz bars rather than barrister's chambers.

AC: When we first met, we discussed your personal stylistic influences and how they've informed what you do at Spencer Hart.

NH: I grew up in the 1970s and my musical interests were imported soul and jazz: Roy Ayres, Donald Byrd and the Crusaders. At the time, a lot was going on in the UK that was driven by music, the Teds followed by Mods, Skins and Soul Boys, various tribes. England has had a special relationship with black American music, jazz in particular, since the 1940s. I had a friend who introduced me to the stylistic influences as well as the music – the pared-down look of Be-Bop, and the Brooks Brothers suits, simple white shirts and skinny ties of Miles Davis and John Coltrane. It was a radical approach, taking aspirational, white-middle-class clothes and re-appropriating them. It was the basis of the Soho Mod style, and, to me, there's something larger than life about it that I have always found very attractive. These people created their own universes by taking traditional ideas and distorting them, using them out of context, exaggerating their meaning.

AC: The early East Coast jazz movement and British Mod style have clearly had a strong influence on you.

NH: In my teens, one friend was a punk, I was a Soul Boy, I had another friend who was a Mod and my best friend, Spencer, was the son of a Be-Bop musician. It was Spencer who introduced me to the differing worlds of Dexter Gordon, Miles Davis, Louis Jordan and Cab Calloway, and, later on, skat musicians, like Eddie Jefferson, who were the founders of rap. I loved the humour, the recurring themes of men who were constantly in trouble, looking sharp and gambling at

Bar Italia, Frith Street (left) and Berwick Street Market (right), London. The streets of Soho provide the backdrop for the playing out of Mod culture.

the racetrack, always making a big entrance. They seemed to have misplaced priorities, like going to parties with their own records and a change of clothes, but they were also well-read and charming. They had a sixth sense about style, knew which rules to break. I think the Teds were also important to the development of my style, because they took the traditional Savile Row block and made it their own, made it slightly threatening. Of course, a lot of that personal investment and interpretation happened because they couldn't get top tailors to make for them due to cost, but I also think there was an importance given to the fact the clothes came out so directly from the context of these people's lives, that there was a certain appropriation involved. Spencer Hart is part Teddy Boy distortion and part fantastical, Bowie-esque Soul Boy. My inspiration is varied, traditional but with a fantastical quality, because, in my opinion, great menswear comes out of a narrow design brief otherwise the clothes look over-designed; all these people understood where the parameters were and how to remix the ingredients to make something new. More than anything, my reference point is music.

AC: What is the spirit of Spencer Hart?

NH: Quality and modernity: the perfect black suit, the perfect white shirt. Spencer Hart is about individualism, stealth wealth and subtle luxury. The mission is to create a product that packs a lot of attitude, but in a subtle way. Style has to appear effortless, natural and understated, never trying too

hard, and yet have that indefinable something, a richness of fabric and meaning that separates that person from the next. It's distinctive, but coded. Jude Law has style, an old-school decadence, sense of distortion and ability to mix old and new. I've been affected by my experiences, and over the last twenty years I've loved Armani's early work for companies like Bagutta, it was revolutionary; Commes des Garçons in the late 1980s; Prada menswear in the first two years; Jil Sander, again for the first two years; and, of course, British bespoke. I also try and inject some British humour into the work; we go to enormous lengths to get the product absolutely right, but it's important to remember they are clothes to feel good and to live in. You're in a nightclub, it's 4am and you're on the dance floor cutting a dash. Rather than take your jacket off, you do up the middle button because it looks good, and looking good is far more important than comfort. Comfort is over-rated. Feeling sharp and being witty, dancing to great music and one-liners flying – this is comfort. It's the difference between being hip and being straight, between Mick Jagger and Paul McCartney. I think dandyism comes in non-conformity, and I've always been drawn to the rebel.

Mourad Mazouz, restauranteur, at work, Sketch, Conduit Street, London.

Opposite: Yann Debelle de Montby, director of image and press relations at Alfred Dunhill Ltd, in the store, Jermyn Street, London.

Below: Tom Baker, tailor, on the rooftop, Soho, London.

Opposite: Nick Hart, tailor, in the West Bar at
Sketch, Conduit Street, London.

Below: Guy West, cobbler, on St James's
Street, London.

Below: Raoul Shah, joint managing director
of Exposure (a brand marketing consultancy),
on Hampstead Heath, London.

Opposite: David Piper, party organizer,
performer and inventor, in Shoreditch Park,
London.

Below: Raoul Shah, joint managing director of Exposure (a brand marketing consultancy), on Hampstead Heath, London.

Below: Olaf and Tim Parker, design director and commercial director of Burro, in the showroom, Brewer Street, London.

Opposite: Eddie Prendergast, managing director of The Duffer of St George, in Shoreditch, London.

Opposite: Kristian Aadnevik, designer, on his
way to work, Chelsea, London.

Below: Mark Ogus, musician, at home,
Bethnal Green, London.

Below: Mat Bickley, designer and promoter,
at home, Hackney, London.

Opposite: Stephen Coates, musician,
in Hackney, London.

East End Flâneur

Rooted in a flamboyant urban camouflage, the East End Flâneur
is a media-savvy neo-bohemian.

The Flâneur, as portrayed by Charles Baudelaire and, following him, Walter Benjamin, was an urban voyeur, an individual who lived life on, and inspired by, the streets. Much of the contemporary debate around fashion and dress has focused on the importance of environment, of a particular location, as a source of creative inspiration. Beau Brummell's dandyism was as much informed by the locale in which he lived and played as it was by any broader socio-political context. In the twenty-first century, London's industrial district in the east is at the heart of a trajectory of oppositional style that began in Soho in Brummell's period. Conversely, it was the very lack of any obvious outlet for consumer consumption that attracted the East End's creative community, drawn there by the large working studios and comparatively cheap rents. Pushed out of the centre by the increasing domination of global brands, young designers, stylists, publishers, artists, musicians and DJs found the East End an environment in which they could investigate their growing frustration with the pervasive and homogeneous culture of mid-1980s England. Characterized by high-rise blocks and crumbling warehouses, the East End was a blank, definitively urban wasteland on which they could build an alternative and insistently non-conformist culture.

East End dandyism unsurprisingly manifests itself in numerous ways, from the quasi-military iconography of a functional ostentation, through the revival of vintage branded goods and bohemian lifestyles to an aesthetic stemming from the extravagant sartorial style of rock outsiders. All are influenced by their context – a potent cocktail of back-street tailors, glass-fronted city banks, dive bars, flower markets and the area's darker history of violent confrontation, gangsters, gambling, boxing and the seductive pleasures of the music hall and prostitution – in an intense and passionate engagement with the realism of urban life.

One branch of the East End style from the late 1990s to early 2000s was rooted in a flamboyant urban camouflage. Design companies like Maharishi, Vexed Generation, Griffin and 6876 produce what fashion theorist and curator Andrew Bolton has described as 'supermodern clothing…designed to respond to the physical and psychological demands of transitional spaces such as roads, railways, airports and the street',[1] redeploying military-tested fabric and styling, blade and slash cutting and camouflage prints, turning the tools of the establishment against themselves. These brands are political in their outlook, the work conceived in subtle but pointed opposition to a growing national 'terror' psychology perpetuated in the media and by government. Not simply about the physical protection of the individual wearer, these clothes were intended to protect the idea of the individual from the homogenizing influence of state invasion. As designer Jeff Griffin suggests:

We conform to nothing, we rebel, we offer something alternative, something personal. I would call that dandy.

Opposite, left: Jarvis Cocker at the Turner Prize awards (9 December 2001). Cocker has been described by writer and former MP George Walden as an archetypal contemporary dandy; he is also a central figure in the Hoxton revolution.

Opposite, right: Hoxton Square. A focal point for the area's cultural renaissance, the square is lined with seminal bars (Blue Note, Shoreditch Electricity Showroom) and galleries (White Cube 2), as well as the studios of famous artists and designers. Artist Joshua Compton used the square as the canvas for 'A Fête Worse Than Death' (1994), which marked the turning point in the area's transformation.

Right: Griffin Creed, Autumn/Winter 01/02.

Far right: 'Shark' coat by Vexed Generation, Autumn/Winter 99/00. Launched in response to government proposals to tackle public disorder, Vexed Generation became synonymous with designs that protected the wearer from both rising crime and the perceived invasion of personal freedom parliamentary bills would entail. The 'shark' coat can be zipped up to conceal the wearer's face from surveillance cameras and is made from ballistic nylon – the same material as bullet-proof vests.

Come in from the Cold

We're a shot in the arm, the rebels of charm. Too much of what's out there's disposable: They're in it for a minute, We're in it to win it –
True

And it's not just about the fabric, so much of what we do is who we hang with, how we speak, how we feel, art, music, video – this is our work, rest and play....

Griffin is about coming from within, it's how you begin, the space you're in and right now that's right here...

Griffin's creed (above) is resonant of that of the nineteenth-century Flâneur, whose performance and practice was equally lived out on the streets. Walter Benjamin's epic *The Arcades Project* sets out the principles of the Flâneur and echoes the Griffin creed:

In our standardized and uniform world, it is right here, deep below the surface, that we must go. Estrangement and surprise, the most thrilling exoticism, are all close by.[2]

Much of that depth in the twenty-first century is found in collaboration; working with illustrators, animators, film-makers, curators, graphic and product designers, artists, poets, the modernity of these brands is rooted in the resulting creative energy and innovation.

Philosopher Michel Foucault, writing on Baudelaire, suggested that, 'Modern man...is not the man who goes off to discover himself...he is the man who tries to invent himself,'[3] and originality remains crucial for the East End Flâneur. Nineteenth-century dandy Oscar Wilde once said, 'One should either be a work of Art, or wear a work of Art' and the East End Flâneur is the ultimate expression of the music, fashion and art trinity that characterizes English street style today. It is this focus on originality and personal identity that forms the sole link between these supermodernists and another feature of the East End Flâneur, which tallies more closely with the eccentric, 1960s rock surrealism of Viv Stanshall and the performance art of Alfred Jarry and Leigh Bowery. Critic Michael Bracewell makes the link between the East End, its art and bohemianism:

There is the sense that one has crossed the width of a street and exchanged the soft-lapelled opulence of banking for a breeding ground of bohemianism... The very idea of [the East End's] high-speed, DIY, hit-and-run art-making... was seen as a miniaturised version of punk rock's cultural revolution: an overturning of the old established order by young, fast, sharp and shocking artists.[4]

Although bohemianism has manifested itself in disparate ways over the centuries, the prevailing similarity between the strands has been to strive toward what sociologist Elizabeth Wilson describes as the 'collapse of art into life', the repositioning at the centre of artistic practice those aspects of the everyday that have always been considered peripheral: 'dress, surroundings and relationships'.[5] It is surely no coincidence that so much of the energy around contemporary British art is located in the East End,[6] with it history of industrial production; that so much of that art deals with the everyday; and, in turn, that the links between art and dress in this area have been and remain strong. Artists such as Gilbert & George and Tracey Emin (represented by Jay Jopling's White Cube), are as famed for the construction of their image through clothing as they are for locating themselves and their surroundings at the centre of their work.

The relationship between the bohemian and the dandy is hotly debated, as Matthew Glamorre argues below. But, many characteristics remain shared. The East End Flâneur draws on the role of the individual in modern, capitalist society; the considered construction of individuality through dress; the high-energy, DIY remaking of the self as a work of art – a gesture argues Wilson, 'characteristic of bohemianism'[7] – fuelled and inspired by a generation of visual artists with shared concerns. The location is also vital: an area in which all these issues are explored daily, on the street and in microcosm, then projected outward, at rapid speed, by a voracious media in regular search of new ideas, causing the search for originality to begin again.

Interview with Neil Boorman

Neil Boorman was the publisher of *Shoreditch Twat*, the cult abrasive fanzine now synonymous with east London's creative scene. He went on to edit *Sleaze* magazine and write a weekly column for *The Guardian's Guide* before launching monthly lifestyle magazine *Good For Nothing*.

AC: When did you first start working in east London?
NB: Eight years ago. Soho was completely finished, and it seemed as though Hoxton was about to emerge; the Blue Note had taken over from the Bass Clef and all the good parties were happening in that area.
AC: What has changed since then?

NB: People's perceptions. It was an awful one-way system with an indigenous population of working-class families eking out a living. So much has changed since then; eight years is a short time in London for an area to be so totally regenerated. There have been various different waves of change – from the artists and creative companies who first drew attention to the place, through to Hoxton as a catch all for trendy London, to now, somewhere where people who want to be cool and trendy go and wonder where all the cool people are. That process has been driven by the media, by the idea of Cool Britannia, and the area has become representative of a generation of cultural London.
AC: It seems that the relationship between music, fashion, art and publishing is crucial to this area.
NB: One of the main reasons people came here was because it was cheap; the council was offering low rents to people who were creatively based, young upstart companies – it certainly wasn't for the scenery. But that generated a much more DIY, grass-roots, organic view of business, a sense that you could make a go of it because the basics were as cheap as chips and yet you were so close to the centre.
AC: It strikes me that the local style has changed massively in the last two years from urban camouflage to a much more bohemian glam-rock, music-inspired thing. How have you seen styles change over the years?
NB: Everything was much more androgynous, that urban utility wear meets high-tech sportswear look. It's gone from that to embrace heroin chic, the beginnings of an

Opposite, left and middle: Griffin, Autumn/
Winter 04/05 collection.
Opposite, right: The Bricklayers Arms.
The pub played a central role in the
development of Hoxton's nocturnal culture
for the creative community.

Below: 'Stencil Boy', *Shoreditch Twat* (2001).
The fanzine was launched by club promoter
Neil Boorman and graphic designers BUMP as a
satire on the way in which the area had become
a caricature of itself in the late 1990s.

Right: Shoreditch Electricity Showroom, Hoxton Square. Trained architect Seng Watson launched this bar and restaurant in 1997. The wide-open spaces of the ground-floor bar provided the perfect platform for the early Hoxton dandy swagger.

Opposite: Dream Bags, Jaguar Shoes, Kingsland Road, London. A later entrant in the Hoxton bar scene, Dream Bags is the ideal place to spot a new generation of Shoreditch creatives.

attempt to move towards rock'n'roll culture. That shift has partly come from the Bridge and Tunnel first-timers misappropriating the utility style with those ridiculous, oversized mullets that have spilled over into the rest of the country and beyond into Europe – a haircut with a life of its own. It is hard to be individual in this context, when you can buy yourself into Shoreditch at Top Shop for under a hundred quid.

AC: How and why did the *Shoreditch Twat* come about?
NB: It happened because we had thousands of people walking through the 333, the club we were doing, and we were frustrated that we couldn't communicate with them in any other way than by playing records. Hoxton was changing and we needed an outlet to express views on how it was changing; the DIY approach was appropriate to the area.

AC: What is *Good For Nothing* responding to?
NB: The first thing is it's free. By distributing in non-magazine places, it goes straight to the people we want to reach, avoids censorship and is a lot more immediate – I think people genuinely want that. They are yearning for something that is less international, more parochial, something of their back yard. You are defined by the sandwich you eat, offered a guide to the best toilets when caught short in London, plied with as many of the unattractive elements of living in a big city like London as you are with the more glamorous ones. It's just honest. *Good For Nothing* reflects street-level aesthetics and values, a down-to-earth attitude towards work, play and life in general.

AC: Do you see anything dandy in the way you dress?
NB: I've never attempted to be part of those micro-trends that Hoxton is adept at generating, I couldn't think of anything worse, and I've never understood it. I'm not a maverick style pioneer, but I do spend a lot of time and effort making sure I don't look like the guy standing next to me in the pub. I'd like to think that anyone who is a true a dandy wouldn't sit around and think about whether they were or not. Dandyism is completely related to the environment you're in: if I was in Bromley High Street, I'd be beaten up, but in Hoxton I probably wouldn't, but would find it comparatively difficult to define myself sartorially as an individual. It's all about context.

Interview with Matthew Glamorre

Matthew Glamorre (see p. 13) is a club promoter, producer and performer, most recently with The Siren Suite. He launched club night Kash Point at the Thames river venue Tattershall Castle in 2001. It has marked a resurgence of political dandyism in the capital.

AC: Brummell's political philosophy, so it is said, was to stand for nothing in particular, yet you clearly state that dandyism is 'socio-political confrontationism through appearance'. How do you equate what seem to be two vastly differing positions?
MG: Firstly, Beau Brummell was a wit at the turn of the

nineteenth century, a time so intensely politicized that the whole of Europe was on the brink of revolution. True 'dandies' are contrary and satirize their times, leaders, public and politics. To stand for 'nothing in particular' was not an option for the English aristocracy during the French Revolution. Brummell's stated philosophy is in true dandy fashion, flippancy at a time of urgency. It's designed for maximum effect and is a successful sound-bite that has travelled through his time and down to ours. Great dandies are endlessly quotable and understand self-promotion: personality, appearance and reputation in the right amounts equal mythical status. The myth is the currency.

AC: Brummell said 'If John Bull should turn to look at you, you are not well-dressed; but either too stiff, too tight or too fashionable.' Clearly, the whole point of what you do is that John Bull should turn to look at you. It strikes me that your practice, like that of Leigh Bowery, has much more to do with Wildean polemics than Brummellian restraint.

MG: Brummell's was a pointedly political revolt against the elaborate French fashions of the day. His sober style was, to me, a socio-political statement of anti-French, anti-flamboyance and anti-fashion, displaying the contrariness that is central to the dandy. Just because he espoused 'dressing down' does not remove him from the lineage, instead it confirms him as a true agent of social, aesthetic and political change.

Oscar Wilde, on the other hand, was in revolt against conservative Victorian society, his extravagance was controversial and desirable in its conspicuousness. Edith Sitwell once said, 'Eccentricity is not…a form of madness. It is often a kind of innocent pride, and the man of genius and the aristocrat are frequently regarded as eccentrics because genius and aristocrat are entirely unafraid of, and uninfluenced by, the opinions and vagaries of the crowd.'

This contempt for common ignorance and its indulgence by authority, the media and religion motivates many dandies. The drive to separate, or rise above, is often born from feelings of rejection and/or attack. Some people are just different. In today's world of mass conformity, promoted by the powerful mind manipulation of consumer corporations, to stand out is more perilous than it has been for many years.

AC: For Karl Marx and Walter Benjamin, the dandy and the bohemian were on the same trajectory. How much of the bohemian is there in what you do?

MG: Dandies are true revolutionaries, philosophers and artists who, from their outsider position, observe and comment upon a shared 'reality'. A true bohemian on the other hand enjoys the 'bon vivant' and daily confrontation is not to their taste. Although they often perform as cogs within the wheels of change, they rarely lead the way. Humour, colour, flamboyance and intelligence combine to make the dandy what he is – at once ridiculed and revered – a jester and a sage. Dandies are immaculately personalities: prophets, poets and pariahs.

'A day in the life of' by hairstylist and dandy
James Main. This series was commissioned for
The New English Dandy as a photo-diary of an average
day in a dandy's life, demonstrating the
important blend of dress, art and performance.
Sam Taylor-Wood is on the decks as Boy George and
Nigel Coates look on.

Martin Green, club promoter, in Bethnal Green
Working Men's Club, London.

Luca Cazal, guitarist in The Cazals,
outside his house, London.

Johnny Vercoutre, proprietor of Time for Tea,
in Shoreditch, London.

Neil Boorman, magazine publisher,
in his home, London.

Barry 7, member of the group Add N (to X) and
antique dealer, at Carnesky's Ghost Train, London.

Phil Bush, lead singer with The Cazals,
at The Griffin Public House, London.

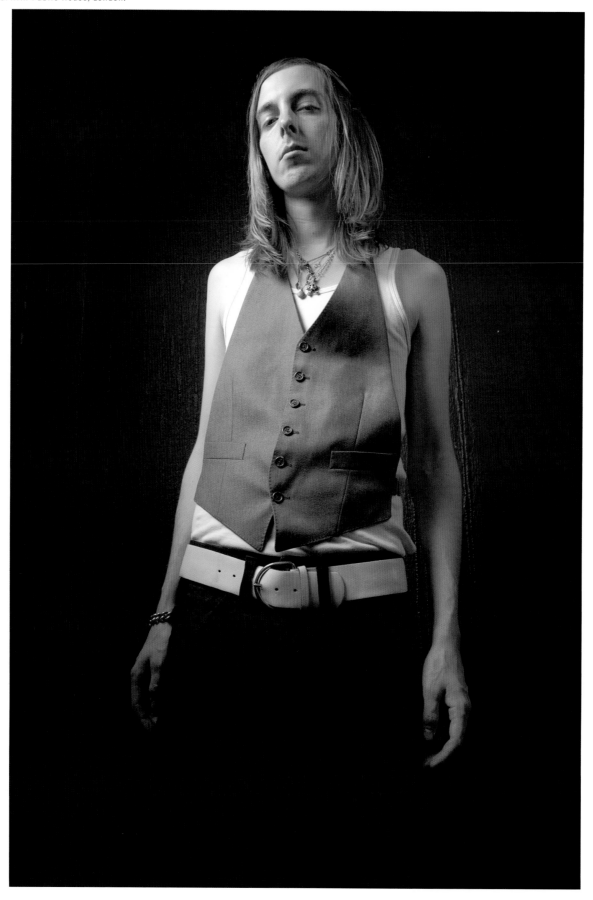

François Nordmann, vintage clothing dealer and
DJ, outside his house, London.

Dexter de Leádús, shopkeeper,
in Leadenhall Place, London.

Liam Casey, singer with Paloma and the
Penetrators, on Kingsland Road, London.

Alastair Mackinven, guitarist with The Country
Teasers & Cünst, outside his studio, London.

Jonathan Wooster, cabaret artiste,
on his roof, London.

Richard Clouston, club promoter, on Highbury
Crescent, London.

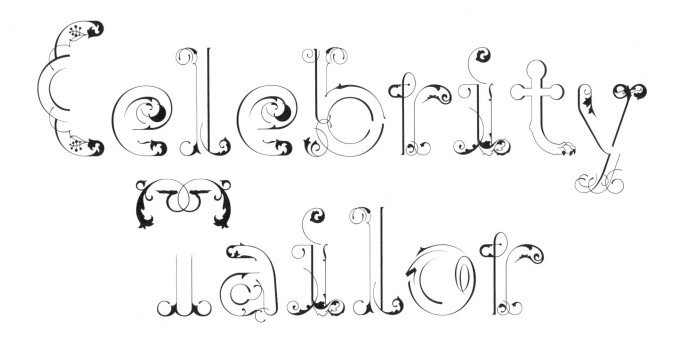

Celebrity Tailor

Vibrant colour, sparkling fabric, the art of cut and embellishment and the mastery
of individual tailors create the ultimate masculine physique.

Right: David and Victoria Beckham at the MTV Movie Awards in Los Angeles (31 May 2003). Beckham has almost single-handedly affected a revolution in masculine dress in Britain. He is acutely aware of the importance of his appearance in the development of his celebrity status.

Opposite: Ozwald Boateng, Spring/Summer 2003 collection. Boateng closed Savile Row for this catwalk show to launch his new studio on the famous street. The show attracted over 2000 people, including the Mayor of London, Ken Livingston, who wore a custom-made Boateng suit.

Whilst gentlemanly tailoring is traditionally shrouded in anonymity and discretion, the industry has also attracted a number of tailors who have deployed their personal charisma as a marketing tool. The first Celebrity Tailor was Henry Poole, who, in 1846[1] gathered around him a clique of political, artistic and literary glitterati, his studio as much a salon and meeting place as a fitting room. Poole used his own notoriety to attract his clientele and it is a method many have adopted since. Henry Poole & Co. still exists at 15 Savile Row, but it is the newer entrants, Richard James and Ozwald Boateng, along with their Soho counterparts, Mark Powell and John Pearse, who have assumed the original Mr Poole's mantle.

There have been many in between, most notably in the 1960s when style began to outpace quality as the principal concern for a generation of conspicuous consumers. When style is the distinguishing factor, the taste and integrity of its arbiters is of paramount importance. Rupert Lycett-Green (Blades) on Dover Street, John Stephen (His Clothes) on Carnaby Street, Simon Boyle (Allsopp, Brindle & Boyle) on King's Road and Michael Fish (Mr Fish) on Clifford Street played as much on their own credibility as style icons as on the consistently high quality of their product. However, it is interesting to note that they were entrepreneurial retailers rather than trained tailors. Of the more traditional houses, it was Louis Stanbury, brother of Kilgour's Fred, who fostered Poole's belief in the importance and power of personal celebrity. Stanbury

was considered 'wild', using his own name on collections for Selfridges and launching a diffusion boutique, Number Ten, on Dover Street specifically catering for a generation who had grown up in the teenage boom but had outgrown the cheaper frivolities of the standard Carnaby Street emporiums. Meanwhile, Kilgour had its own celebrity patrons, most notably Cary Grant, and Louis Stanbury exercised his astute public relations to achieve success, playing on a heady mix of the parent company's client list, the general obsession with style and his own innate ability to predict it.

It was another trained tailor, Tommy Nutter, and his partner Edward Sexton who truly revolutionized the Row, opening at 35a on 14 February 1969. The twenty-six-year-old Nutter had met and impressed his backers (Peter Brown, an executive at The Beatles' Apple Records, lawyer James Vallance White and entertainer Cilla Black) at a Mayfair nightclub, and they brought with them not only money but also clients, most famously Bianca Jagger and The Beatles. Nutter was the stylist while Sexton ran the cutting room, and the House of Nutter set out to be the place 'where you could get design elements, which was the last thing any tailor would want to do because you went to Savile Row not to be noticed'.[2] Nutter and Sexton absolutely intended to be noticed and installed a plate-glass window front, the first on the Row, to open up the hallowed halls to full view of the public. Nutter moved with ease between 'the transience of the society night-club and the solidity of the cutting-room table,

between public spectacle and private craft',[3] his brilliance lying in the ability to strike a perfect balance between fashion (the exterior projection of style) and high-quality, traditional craftsmanship (the construction of the perfect celebrity body).

Tommy Nutter has certainly influenced Mark Powell, who often draws on postwar London, Teds and Carnaby Street of the 1960s. The Mark Powell spirit is traditional tailoring infused with street style:

It's definitely a London thing, gangsters and Pearly Kings, vaudeville and Savile Row. The gangster is the most obvious influence, but there's a lot drawn from the postwar streets, the Duke of Windsor and Hollywood musicals from the 1930s.

Powell's own style is very considered, inflected with East End hoodlum chic, but he accepts:

My personality and personal look are incredibly important; they can also be dangerous. People often interpret the way I dress as being the image of the brand, and although it would be true to say, like Nutter, that there's an essence of my style in the cuts I choose, it's definitely reinterpreted for other people's tastes. My clients are often influenced by celebrity looks, but the feeling of largesse you get from bespoke is more to do with the look and feel of the suit, the body language changes. It's like sheep in wolves' clothing. Tailoring is the perfect way to create individuality;

it's a very non-conformist route. Casual fashion just homogenizes – it's all made in the same factories – and this has had a big influence on the emergence of the new dandy, an increased interest in tailoring with an edge.

Like Powell, Boateng often bemoans the popular misconception that his clothing only suits men who share his physique. His appointment in 2003 as creative director at the Parisian house of Givenchy suggests that the potentially broad appeal of his trademark sharp-cut, vividly colourful suiting has finally been acknowledged. The fit is a neat one; Boateng has described himself for years as a bespoke couturier for whom the equal marriage of craft and design is vital in the development of his signature style:

It was Tommy Nutter who showed me how suits should be. Then, I started visiting the different places where the shoulders and the collars were made, watching and learning the processes. Because I was self-trained, I could question the methods of working and, as I learned the skills, I also learned to adapt them.

Boateng has an innate ability to play with colour – from the peacock hues of his house style to the more subtle tones of his work for Givenchy – combined with lithe, whippet-thin elegance of line. No stranger to celebrity, he has a stellar client list (Samuel L. Jackson, Russell Crowe) and was involved in the movies *Matrix Reloaded* (2003), *Tomorrow Never Dies* (1997) and *Alfie* (2004).

Right: Detail of the interior of Ozwald Boateng's store on Vigo Street, London. The interiors, in both the store and Savile Row studio, reflect the vibrant colour and flamboyance of Boateng's label.

Far right: John Pearse postcard. Pearse's suits may appear quite traditional on the exterior, but trademark rainbow snakeskin linings hint at rebellion. Pearse was also one of the first tailors to experiment with suits in such materials as cord and denim. He sends regular postcards to his client database to notify them of new collections.

Opposite: Lounge Lover bar and restaurant, London. In its early days, Lounge Lover was the perfect venue for celebrities at leisure with its opulent grandeur hidden behind an unassuming façade. The floor rises gently towards the VIP area at the end of the bar, perfectly framing the celebrity clientele in a halo of neon and crystal.

Boateng is as self-assured as his clients are famous:

My father told me I was named Ozwald after an uncle who lived his life according to his instincts and intuition. I always knew I would make it.

John Pearse also recognizes the importance of his image and personality to the success of the label'. He completed his apprenticeship at Hawes & Curtis (1961–64), 'doing a McQueen on the suits', and opened Granny Takes a Trip in 1965. The store, like Michael Rainey's neighbouring Hung on You, and, later, Vivienne Westwood and Malcolm McLaren's Let It Rock (all three on the King's Road), defined a generation of subcultural street style with its trademark, big-fronted shirts, military jackets, moon-jetted pockets and 1940s double-breasted chalk-stripe suits. Pearse opened John Pearse in 1986; whilst his tailoring style retains very little of the Trip spirit, flashes remain in the accessories. He sees himself principally as a creative stylish tailor:

Unlike a designer, I don't have to shift volume and, most importantly, I can respond to a client's individual needs. So if I have a signature style, it's that there is no signature style. I'm a citizen of the world and my clients respond to that.

For Pearse, the dandyism is in the attention to detail, the quality and fit, 'all else will follow'.

Importantly, it is not just these tailors' talent for generating their own celebrity but also their ability to create it for their clients that has made London a centre for tailoring of this kind. The art of tailoring is the ability, through sleight of hand and mastery of proportion, to perfect and refine a client's physique. However, the 'London Look' – narrow, flat-fronted trousers and slim-fitting, waisted jackets – particularly favours the kind of sporting frame that, through its association with nobility and prowess, has over the centuries been afforded an inherent moral superiority. It is no coincidence then that London's Celebrity Tailors are gaining increasing notoriety in a century obsessed with stardom as much conferred by beauty as by talent. For those lucky enough to be born with muscularity and stature, the style serves to emphasize this; for those not so fortunate, these tailors are accomplished practitioners of flattery and illusion.

Richard James in conversation with Christopher Breward

The designer-retailer Richard James has been at the forefront of a turnaround in the fortunes and status of classic English tailoring. Based at the epicentre of the trade in Savile Row, James's shop provides a sleek and innovative take on a style of dress that has defined masculine fashion on the international stage for over two centuries. Paying homage to the sharp edge that the best of Savile Row suits have always maintained,

James's location in the Row is deliberate. But, his style and appeal have moved beyond the Row's traditional customers to attract a wide range of new clients, including music and film-industry performers and executives, advertising and design creatives, even museum directors and academics. The open atmosphere of his shop is inviting, free of the daunting exclusivity associated with some of James's older neighbours, and his deft use of colour, print and beading bestows some subtle dazzle on a traditional industry. Richard James was named British Fashion Council Menswear Designer of the Year in 2001.[4]

CB: In the course of your career how did you move from graphic design to photography, through fashion buying and merchandising, to menswear design?
RJ: I left Brighton with a degree in graphic design. I had specialized in photography and wanted to be a fashion photographer, but didn't know a thing about fashion. I saw a sign in the window of Browns in South Molton Street that said 'sales person required'. Browns, then, was the most fabulous fashion store in the world. I went for an interview, got the job and stayed there for ten or twelve years. I forgot about being a fashion photographer because I got hooked on clothes and on the glamour of what was happening in that world.

I'm not a technician, I'm not a tailor, I'm a retailer. If people ask me, I always say I'm a shopkeeper, and Browns gave me the perfect grounding. In the end though, during the 1980s, I realized I was looking for

clothes for my customers that I couldn't find anymore. I was looking for classic clothes but we were in the period of fashion where labels dominated. If you were wearing Armani, people would really know you were wearing Armani. Yet there were people wanting classic clothing but there wasn't the sort of classic available that resonated with younger people.
CB: For that generation of consumers the notion that you could buy something that was individual was new. The brand was so predominant by the mid-1980s that it was all about acquiring labels and not about the mobilization of individual taste.
RJ: Yes. We're now in a period of globalization. The big brands are huge and you can buy Prada and Gucci not only in every capital city, but in four or five locations in some of those cities; they're too available now. So people are reacting against globalization and are much more informed about what they want. Individuality is the be-all and end-all at the moment.
CB: How would you describe the characteristics of your brand and its evolution?
RJ: My business partner Sean Dixon and I decided we should open our own shop. We had both worked at Browns, and retailing was our history and experience and has remained our bedrock. What better place to open a shop than the centre of individuality that is Savile Row? We wanted to do beautiful classic clothes, clothes where fifty per cent of the cost wasn't going towards an advertising budget, clothes that were based on being English but modern. The clothes were value for

Right: Richard James, Savile Row. The use of a full glass façade, reminiscent of Tommy Nutter's studio, was still revolutionary when James entered the Row in the early 1990s.

Far right: Richard James advertising, Spring/Summer 2005. James is acutely aware of the importance of extending his design vision across all elements of his label. Whilst this is a common approach for most brands, it is fairly unusual for a Savile Row establishment to effectively communicate its image and identity in this way.

money, the fabrics were beautiful, the make was beautiful and everything about them was as it should be. In a way what we do is a caricature of what I think Savile Row style is: the nipped-in waist and longer jacket, the natural shoulder. Our silhouette is English, it can only be English. It comes across as being very lean except it's not, it's just the cut of the jacket that gives that appearance.

CB: All your raw materials and labour are sourced in the UK. Do you deliberately set out to promote British products or companies?

RJ: It's not necessarily that we feel we have to do things that are British, but our product is British and we're located in a very British street. We have developed relationships with mills in Yorkshire, probably the best in the world, and we go there and design fabrics ourselves. We can buy relatively small quantities of things that are very special. To be able to say that we've bought sixty metres of this fabric and we'll make ten bespoke suits and twenty ready-to-wear suits and that's the end of it, goes back to the issue of individuality. It's the opposite of globalization, and I think that is so important in this day and age.

CB: So the exclusive quality of the textile and attention to detail are central to the Richard James brand?

RJ: Just about every fabric that has a pattern on it we design in some way. We've got a fabric at the moment that is 55% cashmere and 45% wool and it's an 8oz cloth. It's so light but impossible to crease. It's the ultimate luxury suit but it also incorporates the luxury of performance, so it's luxury in the traditional way and it's luxury with a new spirit.

CB: Any discussion of Savile Row involves politics to some degree, and I know that the press have presented your emergence on the scene as a 'scissors at dawn' challenge to an older generation who have been established in the street for years. What's your reaction to that?

RJ: It's funny actually, because Savile Row is an amazing street, a street of quite incredible tailors, and every tailor in the street has got a different point of view, a different way of doing things and a different client base. However, Savile Row is perceived as being out of touch and no longer valid, and certainly for younger people it's an intimidating place to go to. So whenever I'm interviewed I always sing the praises of Savile Row because it is fabulous and the reason I'm there is because it's fabulous and I want to be a part of it. Some of the shops are undoubtedly quite frightening to go into and they're very clubby and very old-fashioned. We decided to do it in a different way by having a shop that is very clean, very light, very modern. We have a product that is as good as anybody else's on the street, but it's presented in a contemporary manner and we're approachable, we're an easy shop to go into.

CB: A lot of your publicity plays on the celebrity client, I don't know if that's by chance or on purpose.

RJ: It's sort of accidental, it's just that we've got these types of people as customers, which we're very lucky to

Murano glass money clip and cuff links by Isabelle Starling. Glass designer Amy Isabelle Cushing and jeweller Ben Starling Day are the creative minds behind Isabelle Starling. Cushing is the first British designer to work with Murano, glass manufacturers to generations of the world's elite. Day's journey as a jeweller has taken him from India via Los Angeles (where he made pieces for the Beverley Hills rich and famous) to Spitalfields, where he now creates pieces for a different kind of creative aristocracy.

have, and they're very happy for us to talk about them. The celebrity thing is very important obviously, although in truth about ninety per cent of our business is making beautiful navy-blue or grey suits. That said, there is something important about the spirit of what we do, which could be associated with celebrity and presentation. Take the camouflage suit, we've been doing that since February 1998 and first made one for a very wealthy gentleman who loved going to the opera but hated wearing suits. He suggested it, we made it and he absolutely loves it. You know, I think what's happened is that the Row became a street of beautiful business suits, but lost its spirit, because Savile Row has traditionally been so individual and so off the wall. The things that Huntsman did in the 1970s were amazing and Tommy Nutter, well, his style was absolutely potty. Even the really traditional ones were doing quite mad things for their customers, but they've lost the client base of people wanting these exquisite, eccentric things. We came to the street with the attitude that we can do anything within the strict confines of traditional tailoring, and I think that creativity always comes through having limitations. The camouflage suits would look stupid if they weren't classic suits. My whole ethic is going to extremes within the boundaries of being classic, and that can be a fluorescent pink cashmere jacket but it's a classic jacket and it's in cashmere, making it fabulous anyway.

Interview with Tom Dixon

Leaving Chelsea College of Art and Design after only six months, Tom Dixon began his career in graphic design and animation in 1980. A year later, he joined Funkapolitan as a bass guitarist and was, for a short spell, a promoter of nightclubs and warehouse parties. He taught himself to weld in 1983, producing furniture as part of the 'Creative Salvage' collection that made his name as a designer. Since then, he has had his work produced by Italian manufacturers Cappellini, launched a retail shop, Space Studio, in Notting Hill, co-founded Eurolounge, which manufactures rotationally moulded plastics and produced a series of commercially successful collections as creative director of UK retailer Habitat. He is currently creative director of Artek, the Finnish furniture manufacturer founded by Alvar Aalto, as well as running a successful business as an independent designer.

AC: The relationship between a tailor and his client is an important one. You've been going to Richard James for a long time now. How did you meet?
TD: I've had a long-standing relationship with Richard since he asked me to make some pieces for his shop in the early 1990s. I was doing a lot of work then for Paul Smith, Vivienne Westwood and Commes des Garçons and I think my collaborations have been closer with fashion designers than anyone else. In my early career, I was

mostly dressed in Savile Row or army surplus – half and half – and operated an elaborate bartering system, where I would exchange work for clothes, giving me access to the British gentleman's kit. I think I probably work more now with Sean (Dixon, James's business partner), but I do still exchange things. I like the fact that the shop's based on Savile Row, going there is a peculiarly British tradition for anyone who fancies themselves as a gent. To say, 'I must introduce you to my tailor' is a classic line when abroad.

AC: What keeps you going back to James's work?

TD: He's got a great take on colour, which isn't easy to do in menswear, and he manages to use classic textiles in a more interesting way than many of his competitors. Richard James is recognized worldwide as a label that epitomizes the classic English look – refined cut, intricate detail – and gives that little bit extra, that colourful lining and additional pockets, which I also think is typically British. There's something great about being measured up properly, especially when you're an awkward shape – long arms, tall and lanky. Going to a British tailor is an experience and quite different from getting clothes in other countries.

AC: Is James's personality crucial to his success?

TD: Well, he uses his network to his best advantage; you can't just be brilliant at what you do anymore. I also can't avoid the feeling that his relationship with celebrities like Elton [John] is very productive; creative people need clients who can both afford their work and understand the significance of what they do. The Row, in particular, needs that otherwise it would vanish. I guess Richard's background in retailing has developed his concern for and interest in his customers.

AC: It's interesting that you describe the celebrity relationship as productive. James mentions in his interview with Christopher Breward that one of his classics – the camouflage evening suit – was first made to request. Have you ever seen any of the pieces you've made together make their way onto the rails?

TD: I'm not sure you can own an idea in that way. Richard comes from a long line of interesting tailors, like Tommy Nutter, who were inspired by the interests and lifestyles of their clients as well as a lineage of influential designers like Scott Crolla, people entering the menswear arena who were using the idea and resource of Savile Row as inspiration. There's an element of it that's a mirage, a front for what is fairly normal fashion design given a hidden depth by its trade on Englishness. Whether it's real or invented, as a consumer you're buying into a tradition that is one end of a massive British industry of garment-making and textiles, even if it's just pattern cutting. And, people are buying into it worldwide.

AC: Do you still buy things off the shelf?

TD: Of course. A mix of Portobello with a Savile Row handmade suit and a smattering of high street is the way to go. Having said that, it's my ambition to have a collection of handmade shoes. It would also be nice to have a butler and be completely made-to-measure, but that's probably unrealistic.

Sebastian Horsley, artist and writer,
wearing John Pearse, in Soho, London.

John Pearse, tailor, in his studio,
Meard Street, London.

Kevin Nolan, musician, wearing Mark Powell,
in Soho, London.

Dylan Jones, editor of *GQ*, wearing Richard
James, in his office, Hanover Square, London.

Tom Dixon, designer, wearing Richard James,
in Spitalfields, London.

Richard Dawson, photographer, wearing Ozwald
Boateng, at home, east London.

Duggie Fields, artist, wearing Ozwald Boateng,
at home, Kensington, London.

Ozwald Boateng's collection (details).

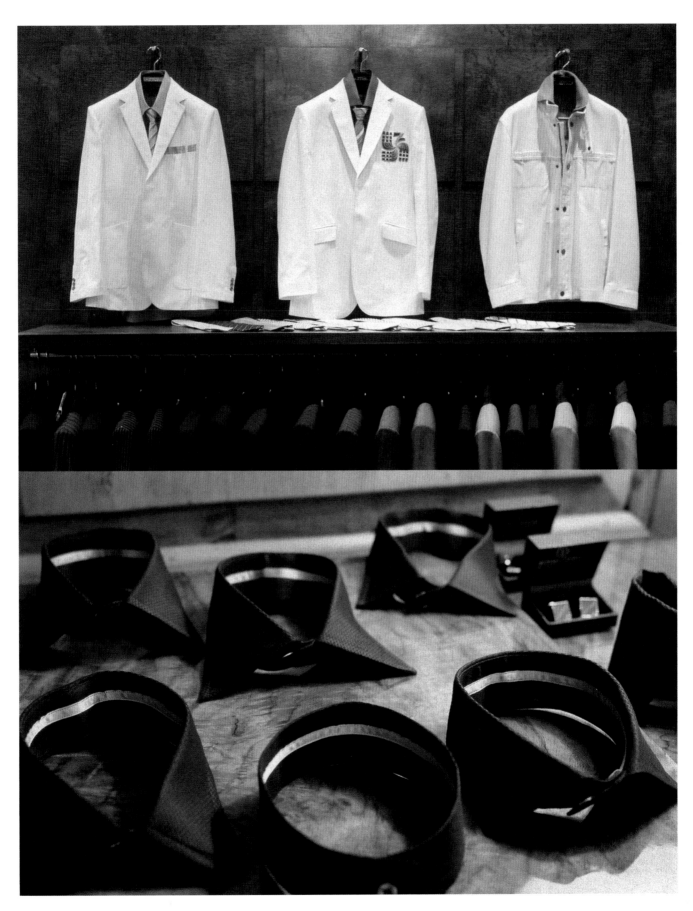

Kerso, accountant, Motherwell, Scotland.

Terrace Casual

Meticulous attention to detail and dedication to functional ostentation positions country and leisure style in the urban environment.

Right and p. 120: 'The New Casuals',
The Renaissance Issue, *i-D* magazine
(no. 207, March 2001). Like many of Britain's
most successful fashion photographers,
Jason Evans, who shot this series, has been
part of the *i-D* stable since the beginning of his
career. Shown here is Toby McLellan, journalist
and garage MC. He wears a leather jacket by
Redskins, shirt by Moschino, jeans by Versace,
umbrella by Armani and Nike Airmax trainers
(total cost £1300).

Opposite, left: Deerstalker hat by Lock & Co.
The deerstalker is one of many symbols of
aristocratic sporting life that the Terrace
Casual has appropriated and made his own.

Mod culture was subsumed by a more mass-market, fashionable imitation in the mid-1960s, and the original Mods began to break apart, drifting into the more florid and feminine fashion of the hippies or hardening into a stark, stripped-down, back-to-basics look informed by two ostensibly conflicting sources, Jamaican Rude Boys and the white working class. These Hard Mods, or Skins, borrowed heavily from the Rudie style — cropped hair, two-tone mohair 'tonic' suits and highly polished brogues — and blended it with traditional working clothes — Dr Martens, bomber jackets, 'union' shirts and shortened, bleached jeans. Class defined the Hard Mod, and in his West Indian neighbours he found the music, style, language and sense of community to express his isolation from and rejection by mainstream, dominant culture. It was a frustration that manifested itself in the extreme violence (quite possibly of a minority) that came to define the Skinhead for the majority of the British public. Paradoxically, the Suedeheads and Smooths of the early 1970s added symbols of the dominant, middle-class city gentleman to the original Skin style — Crombie overcoats, tightly furled umbrellas and bowler hats — in all probability to distance themselves from the overt racism with which Hard Mod culture had become synonymous.

Hard Mods congregated in local youth clubs, on street corners and at the football stadium. In the twentieth century, sport was cultivated as a moral site for the making of national and regional identity and for the transmission to the urban masses of such traditional values as hard work and perseverance. The terraces in particular became a place 'where (predominantly working-class) males forge[d] a communal identity'[1] and, as such, they played a crucial role in the lexicon of Skin culture. In the early 1980s, however, the role of football as a driver for oppositional working-class culture became diluted by a more consumerist subculture. For the new Casual, working-class culture was defined by aspiration, by personal wealth as a measure of success. The Casual's style upheld the aforementioned values that sport was originally intended to embed in the proletariat culture. Morality (one of Brummell's motivating principles) was expressed through immaculate presentation and a faultless attention to detail that bordered on the obsessive. For Brummell, this flawlessness was intended as a means of distinction against the working classes, as fashion historian Christopher Breward notes:

Brummell's celebration of hygiene, clean linen, perfect tailoring and supreme self-control accrued one level of meaning from the contrast between his pampered body and the ragged, emaciated bodies of the poor who littered London's streets.[2]

For the Casuals, the distinction was manifold: to separate themselves from the violence of the Skins, from the punk culture of their brothers and sisters

and, crucially, from the middle classes whose wardrobe they had borrowed and subverted.

Ironically, football played as great a role in facilitating the development of the aspirational Casual as it had in defining the proletarian Skin. It was in the early 1980s, as English football gained a European platform, that fans began to travel more widely to Italy and France. Vehemently patriotic, the national pride of the Casual appeared to be invested as much in the smartening up of Britain's footballing fraternity as in the support of his team. The stark contrast of England's fans to the immaculate dress of their French and Italian counterparts prompted a revolution in working-class style, one dominated by European brands – Fila, Ellesse, Lacoste, Tacchini, Adidas, Stone Island, Slazenger, Fred Perry, Pringle and Lyle & Scott. The Casual embraced the original Mods' internationalist perspective and sartorial 'cool' and combined it with clothing intended for physical pursuit. In the case of the Casual, however, the physical pursuit was that of leisure rather than manual labour, leisure afforded by a wealth and success that had given them access to luxury brands supposedly beyond their means.

Commentators on street style disagree as to whether the 1980s Casual grew out of the Liverpuddlian Scallie from the Scotland Road area or the Mancunian Perries. In the early twenty-first century, however, it is Manchester that is driving a re-discovery of Casual chic. Pringle and Lyle & Scott still feature prominently, but are joined by Norwegian walking gear,

environmentally friendly street-casual clothing, Aquascutum, Burberry and Belstaff. The upper-class sporting pursuits with which these clothes are associated (hunting, shooting, fishing) are redolent of the masculine camaraderie and corporeal engagement of club life favoured by Brummell and his circle. Following Brummell's example, the Terrace Casual is engaged in the positioning of traditional upper-class 'country' style in the urban environment, co-opting it for the pursuit of inner-city leisure rather than the management of rural estates.[3]

Interview with Nigel Lawson and Stephen Sanderson of Oi Polloi

---

In 2002, Nigel Lawson and Stephen Sanderson launched the gentlemen's outfitter, Oi Polloi, in the heart of Manchester's Northern Quarter. Formerly home to the city's rag trade, the area has been regenerated and is now a breeding ground for Manchester's creative community. Lawson has been importing rare Casuals' brands into Manchester for many years and is also the creative director of Elk, an 'ecology-minded street-casual' label. Sanderson is founding director of the MOP hairdressing salon and the Oi Polloi store does haircuts in the basement.

AC: How would you define your style?
SS: It's more about classic design than anything else,

Pages 115 (right)–120 (left): 'Details', a photostory. Meticulous attention to detail and the defining importance of labels that are standard-bearers for functional quality are central to the Terrace Casual. Retailers Nigel Lawson and Stephen Sanderson of Oi Polloi in Manchester (see pp 121 and 128), selected these pieces from the store and their own collections.

classic labels and brands. I'm into things that don't really date. It's a blend of outdoor functional wear with sports casual. I tend to like more traditional waxed fabric and really high-tech Gore-Tex, which to me is the Formula 1 of fabric. There's something flamboyant in knowing how well it performs even if you're never going to use it in extreme contexts. It's like buying a Porsche: you're never going to drive it at full speed. Trainers are crucial, Adidas, Nike, Springcourt, Superga, Vans from the 1970s or early 1980s.

NL: In a word: Quincy.[4] He had the perfect wardrobe: Gazelles in aqua, caramel-coloured Farahs, Harringtons, Catalinas, safari jackets, Lacoste cardigans, Madras-check button-down shirts, deck shoes, cheap yellow fishing jackets, Munsingwear.

AC: The store is called Oi Polloi. Where does it come from?

SS: If you were posh, you would say hoi polloi, meaning the masses, the working classes, and we wanted to make the point that this is a working-class style. We're a traditional gentlemen's outfitter for the masses.

AC: What is it about the Casual style that interests you and how do you see it as relevant today?

SS: As I said, it's the functional aspect of sportswear and outdoor clothing that appeals to me because it's designed to do something rather than to be fashionable. I'm not interested in fashion for fashion's sake. The beauty comes from what the clothing does, the details are all there to do certain jobs and, when you're wearing the best, those details have been

thought out, designed without ugliness. To me that's the link with the Casuals.

NL: I suppose it's also an addiction to expensive clothes that's very similar to the Mod ethos of 1962. Some of those kids had more expensive mohair suits than their bosses. Also, there's a shared love of Italian and French clothing: Italy for shoes and suits, France for Springcourt pumps and merino knitwear. I first got into the Casual thing at eleven and stayed in it until I was seventeen and I guess trainers are the direct connection between what I was wearing then and what I wear now. In terms of sentiment, it was a dress-down movement – jeans, European and American classic clothing, Cerruti crew-neck jumpers, cords and desert boots – but totally considered. You thought about the complete outfit and because of that it was very sharp. Things would be in and out in a month. What I loved about it was the detail. Every single piece of it had to be exact and had to mix, whether you were wearing hunting gear or a full tracksuit. There's not much difference, I hope, between what I was wearing then and what I'm wearing now because those things were, and are, perfect. The biggest difference is that there's less choice. The crucial things are functionality, quality, having the original of the style, colour, form. It's got to look great.

AC: You're quite clear about the importance of 1980s Casual style on what you do. Is there an influence from the Suedeheads and Smooths, the smartening up of Hard Mod style using traditional gentlemanly clothes?

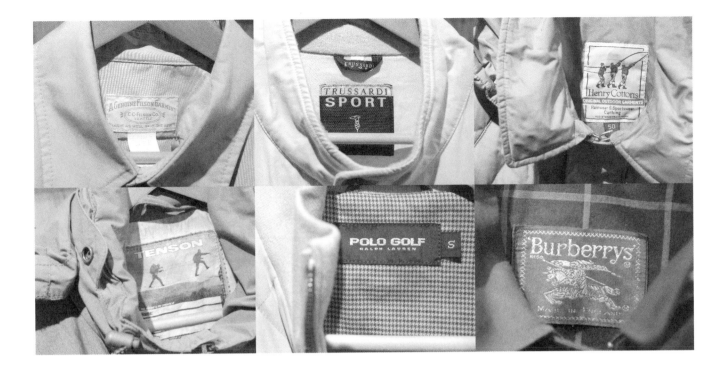

NL: Although the Suedehead movement was more London-oriented, the reasons behind the style and that of the Casuals are exactly the same. I think young working-class men noticed similarities in other cultures from other cities that they could mix with what they were doing. They were taking chances that spiralled out beyond their local context.

SS: The Perry thing also carried through from the Skinhead period, before the Casuals moved onto more luxury brands. To me, wearing brands and carrying the Burberry umbrella are extensions of the Casual approach, the one-upmanship, being a bit flash. The deerstalkers definitely come from that sentiment and look completely different on young urban men with long hair. It is about taking a style and twisting it, turning it into something else.

AC: The Casual style seems inherently dandy to me. Do you agree, and do you see what you're doing as having dandy traits?

NL: Well, it was the last English style movement invented by the people and not by a designer, a band or a magazine.

SS: It was all super, super classic and incredibly subtle – the width of a hem, the collar on a jumper, a logo. It all changed rapidly week by week, from luxury to cheap, and the major part was keeping up with it. You either knew or you didn't, and most people wouldn't have noticed. It's all in the detail, the things that only the other people that know and are into it would recognize. What we do is rooted in working-class culture and that

seems to me to be the biggest difference.

AC: How would you define dandyism?

SS: A slightly obsessive approach to clothing, the refusal to conform, the determination to wear labels that a working-class lad shouldn't normally be wearing. To me, dandies are without social background, they're classless and slip through the net.

NL: A love of tweed, brushed cotton, scarves, jackets, trousers, walking sticks, luggage – all of which Casuals share.

AC: What relationship does football have to what you're doing?

NL: Grandad's ashes are scattered on the pitch at Old Trafford, it's in the blood.

Interview with Jason Evans

Jason Evans has been photographing found sitters for years, his work a comprehensive document of urban, predominantly working-class style. A regular contributor to *i-D*, Evans is one of the principal drivers of the 'Straight-Up' format (full-length, immediate portraits of style setters on the street), a photographic style that has come to define magazine.

AC: What attracts you to found sitters?

JE: A sharp intake of breath usually. If the look is done right, it's really done right – the sense of proportion, volume, fit, all in perfect balance – and can be quite awesome. A large part of my photographic output,

probably around ninety-seven per cent, is street casting and I find something in these people that can't be found using fashion models, who are anaemic for the most part. Their attitude is incredibly inspiring.

AC: What drew you to Casuals as subjects?

JE: There's something incredibly attractive about their considered sobriety. The Casuals of my youth were wearing electric-blue jumbo cords and brightly coloured Perry shirts, which many people would say isn't sober at all, but I think people often get confused about what sobriety means. They associate it solely with the sombre or staid, whereas there is something restrained and understated in the Casuals' stripped-down, bare-bones look that is also excessive and flamboyant. They don't cancel each other out to me.

AC: Do you think there is anything of the dandy in the Casual style?

JE: For me, Casuals are the true contemporary dandies. People assume now that dandy means foppish, but in reality the movement was totally against that. I suppose when you look at Brummell and Baudelaire's cravats from the perspective of the twenty-first century of course they appear frilly, but if you set it in context, what they were doing was utterly minimalist. The Casuals are the same. The term 'conspicuous consumption' is often associated with them, but I don't agree at all. It is inconspicuous consumption, because unless you know the codes, they will pass you by.

Interview with Antony Crook

Antony Crook studied photography in Edinburgh, graduating in 1999. Now based in Manchester, he shoots fashion, advertising and music for ad agencies, design agencies, magazines and record labels in the UK, Europe and America. He also sells his work through galleries. He photographed the sitters in this section.

AC: How did you find these sitters, and what attracted you to the ones you chose?

ACrook: All the people who are into this style know each other, so once I had started to identify people, stories of others began to unfold and, whilst they are mostly based in Manchester, I began to find people rooted in this style in different parts of the country and the continent. Their approach to dress is important; I was looking for meticulous attention to detail. The ones that are featured know exactly what they are wearing and why they are wearing it. Their stance is exceptional, and their ability to put a look together in a certain way – colour, shape, silhouette – is considered and careful in exactly the same way as any other fashionable person, the same as any dandy.

Personalities as much as style suddenly became important when I was shooting; I'd come across a charisma that is difficult to describe, almost like a good band frontman. The clothes are practical, with

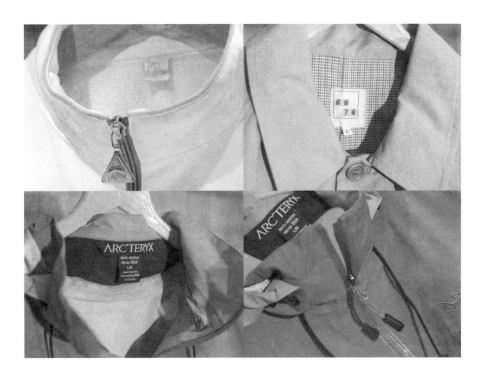

nothing over-designed or unnecessary. All the clothing, the way they wear and buy it, is about functionality – like the Land Rover is 100% function – and they almost surrender aesthetics over purpose, at which point it becomes something beautiful. As soon as the clothes stop being utilitarian, they become a fashion and therefore irrelevant to these people.

When we were shooting, the aim was to be informal, to use the space as if they were waiting for a bus. That their pose or gesture is not directed is consistent with their style. I was looking for simplicity to the stories, I wanted to reflect the modesty they all have about the fact they look good. The stillness of the images really conveys that for me.

AC: You've said you might keep on recording these subjects. What is it about them that has inspired you?

ACrook: When you shoot a lot of fashion and advertising, you're making images that can be dynamic and beautiful, but have no claim on reality at any level. These shots and these people polarize that completely. And that's my favourite kind of photography.

When left to my own devices, I make work that is quiet. I like to capture people simply, to make pictures that whisper and say beautiful things in uncomplicated ways. I think this makes the pictures stronger. It is not something that occurred to me when I started, but the way I photograph is consistent with the way these people are – the opposite of the overt style that many dandies adopt and the way I wanted these people to be seen. Maybe

that's the reason I want to carry on shooting them because it's natural subject matter for my style of photography. The way I edited the pictures, the colours and the composition gently nod towards what the people are wearing, the mood of the shot, drawing out the essence of their look in a clean and simple way. They could have been shot very differently. I could have made them look like hard men, which might have been closer to what some of them would have liked, but there was something very honest and modest about these sitters that I wanted to represent.

AC: Do you think there's anything of the dandy in the Casual style?

ACrook: Of course, because they consider painstakingly what they're wearing, from top to bottom, every day of their lives. They pursue rare items with vigorous determination and employ huge amounts of knowledge. There's a traditional view of the dandy, with the cravat and so on, and the physical look of the Casuals is the opposite, but in the sentiment of dandyism these men are perfect examples. They are very sharp in every aspect of their daily lives. Like the other photographers who worked on this book, I didn't direct people about what to wear or style them in any way because I was keen to read their own style. Because I shot each person over the course of a day, they did bring options, but I was careful to make sure the decisions came from them, nothing is engineered or false.

Far right: 'The New Casuals', The Renaissance Issue, *i-D* magazine (no. 207, March 2001, see p. 114). Dean Scott, stockbroker. He wears a top by Evisu, shirt, cuff links and loafers by Gucci, jeans by Stone Island and watch by Armani (total cost £950).

They even chose the location of the shoot. It's a very subtle thing to make a picture completely honest and if I'd been involved in the selection of the clothing or the location, the validity and accuracy would have been lost.

AC: What do you think links these sitters?

ACrook: Personality and style; what's unique about these men is how personal, how private their style is. A lot of the pieces are specific, rare and expensive, which I found a bit ambiguous because function is intrinsic to these clothes and yet they have become so rare they shouldn't be worn very often or only in certain conditions. But, it's not about showing off – in fact, it's the exact opposite. Shouting about yourself or posing would be extremely uncool. It's about having nothing to prove at all. We never discussed how rare or expensive the clothes are; that was something I found out by showing the pictures to other people. Kerso (see p. 112), for example, has one of the most significant trainer collections in the world but would resist any attempt to be praised or glorified for it. And, in a gesture consistent with and at the essence of all these dandies, he walked down a wet garden path and drove me to the station in a pair of green 1975 Adidas trim masters, to his knowledge the only existing pair in the world.

Nigel Lawson, proprietor of Oi Polloi,
in Chorlton, Manchester.

Chris Day, shopkeeper and collector,
in Barnsley, Yorkshire.

Nick Fry, artist and designer, in the Northern
Quarter, Manchester.

Michael Barnes-Wynters (also known as Barney),
founder of Doodlebug (an international arts
showcase) and visual artist, in Chinatown,
Manchester.

Brownie, vintage clothes dealer, in the
Northern Quarter, Manchester.

Lewi Carroll, publisher, in Hunter's Barbeque,
Manchester.

Rikki Turner, social worker and collector,
in The King's Arms, Salford.

Stephen Sanderson, proprietor of Oi Polloi,
in Ashton-under-Lyne.

Benji Reid, artistic director of Breaking Cycles
(physical theatre), in the Contact Theatre,
Manchester.

Stephen Wilson, promoter, in West Port,
Edinburgh.

Chris Wass, shop owner, in The Phoenix Pub,
Edinburgh.

Gary Smith, art director, at the M6 services,
Knutsford.

Glen Kitson, online clothing dealer,
in Bournemouth.

Steve Cato, DJ and Soul Boy, in Pete's Furniture
Warehouse, Manchester.

Cresser, vocalist, in Manchester.

Andreas
Kronthaler,
design director
at Vivienne
Westwood,
at the florist,
Wandsworth.

New Briton

New and exciting visual languages are made through reflection
on and challenges to cultural heritage.

Right: Captain Vershoyle, Grenadier Guards (1855). Captain Vershoyle was one of the last in a long line of Scots and Englishmen overseas who blended their native dress with the sartorial traditions of the countries in which they found themselves.

Far right: 'Man in Suit' (c. 1970). Nigerian photographer Harry Jacob, who shot this image, made his career taking individual and family portraits of the immigrant population of south London. His work captures a whole generation of London style and was celebrated in an exhibition by curator Alistair O'Neill at the London College of Fashion in 2003.

Without the formal strictures that govern social status in Britain – class, dress, manners and property – there would be little to push against or to explore in its contemporary culture. Britain's puritanical leanings perpetuate bawdiness and revelry at the other extreme, traits that are all part of national tradition. The perception of Britain as reliable, dowdy and conservative affords the perfect stereotype to both celebrate and unravel with each new generation.[1] When designer John Galliano states that 'there are lots of male stereotypes out there. And there's nothing wrong with stereotypes'[2], he no doubt includes the archetypes of English masculinity with which the New Briton plays. Few other national identities offer such enticing challenges, and this chapter explores a dandyism that consciously plays on the archetype of Britishness. In many respects it is a summation of all the typologies addressed in this book because it draws on many of the same references, but it is also a unique strand in its own right as it so deliberately seeks to challenge fixed understandings of what it means to be British in the twenty-first century.

It is a cultural exploration that extends beyond Britain's borders, the twenty-first century so far marked by cultural brooding on a global scale. In an era where national boundaries appear increasingly mutable and nebulous – threatened by the individual ability to delve deeply into the lives and cultures of others through the use of digital and virtual technology, through immigration and emigration and increased,

cheaper travel – societies have responded with mounting levels of national introspection. These self-examinations are repackaged as basic, marketable strap-lines: 'Cool Britannia' and 'India Shining', two of the many, glossy contemporary alternatives to the faded importance of national anthems.

However, as historian and writer William Dalrymple points out in *White Mughals* (part epic romance, part trajectory of cultural fusion), the history of 'early promiscuous mingling of races and ideas, modes of dress and ways of living'[3] between Britain and its former colonies has deep and rich roots, which stand in direct opposition to these rudimentary tag lines. What puts the 'cool' in 'Cool Britannia' are the creative industries of music, art and fashion, which cultural theorist Kevin Davey identifies as the contemporary repositories of national identity, replacing monarchy and parliament as drivers of the nation state. If so, ironically, what is upheld as inherently cool in British identity is the desire to challenge the puritanical island mentally encoded in imperial Britannia. Davey's perceptive analysis of Englishness (rather than Britishness) rightly points to 'transgression, parody, reversal, sexual experiment and downright bad-tempered dissent as important parts of our heritage'[4] and all are characteristics made manifest in British design.

Designers Paul Smith and Vivienne Westwood consistently re-evaluate what it means to be British and how that understanding can be expressed through dress. Smith's work plays on the desires and aspirations

Right: Paul Smith's Westbourne House, Kensington Park Road, London. Paul Smith is the arbiter of a sophisticated and contemporary take on a Britishness redolent of seaside humour and middle-class, rural English lifestyles. It is a combination that has been hugely successful internationally, particularly in Japan.

Far right: Brick Lane, London. The focal point for East End style, Brick Lane is home to Britain's large Bangladeshi community who run the majority of the curry houses for which the street is famous.

of the British bourgeoisie, combining a self-parodying humour with a relentless adoption of international reference (riotous colour, print and embellishment) that evokes the more languid, postwar England of cricket matches and high tea. The resulting collections are as beloved by the descendants of those he simulates as they are by his extensive international audience who respond, principally, to the affection he shows for his subject matter. Westwood exploits a much more urban iconography, mixing the language of elite Western dress (cravats, military regalia, strict tailoring, taffeta, lace) with that of the 'outsider' (tartan, rubber, leather, safety pins, South Asian *shalwar*-style trousers) to create a new language imbued with parody and conflict. As Kevin Davey suggests, Westwood shows are spectacular forums for ideas about history, liberty and national identity, 'startling promenades that rummage deep into English imaginaries, re-inventing the Anglo-British tradition'. Westwood states:

I am English and I parody the English, with the hope that my clothing will have international significance.[5]

Westwood's early work translated and recoded the imperial British character, the strength of which had, in its time, forced the definition of other national identities. With Malcolm McLaren, she produced the infamous 'Which Side of the Bed' T-shirt of loves and hates that pitched John Betjeman, *Vogue*, pop stars, the Arts Council, country living and antiques against

prostitutes, anarchism, pornography and black American culture. But, like Brummell, her affiliation with the urban working class was partial; both punk and the haute couture in which she now trades are rejections of the popular, 'a snob's revenge from on high', and celebrations of society's 'orchids' in opposition to '95% of the people in the world who are weeds and useful plants'.[6] 'Otherness' became, in Westwood's hands, a form of aristocratic distinction – the nobility of style over that of birthright.

In the early 1970s, Westwood and McLaren's 'Buffalo' collection incorporated reworked zoot suits as well as overt references to the emerging ragamuffin. Every serious study of British street style made in the last twenty years has revealed the huge legacy of black American style, personal creativity and innovation on Britain's sartorial landscape. That this look was, in itself, a re-working and interpretation of inspiration afforded by Hollywood cinema, the Sears Roebuck catalogue and various American and British fashion magazines indicates how genuinely difficult it is to identify where national boundaries begin and end when it comes to dress. The Caribbean legacy of domestic dressmaking mirrored, in many ways, Britain's own traditions of make-do-and-mend and back-street tailoring that still prevailed in the era of Windrush and the Teds in the 1950s. Jason Evans and Simon Foxton's 'Strictly' images make this point explicitly. Shot in Northfields – a suburban area of London redolent of the conservative 'bigotry' of middle-English values – the

'Strictly', The High Summer Issue, *i-D* magazine
(no. 94, July 1991). Stylist Simon Foxton and
photographer Jason Evans produced these
images to convey, as Evans states, that
'dandyism is about attitude, not race'.
The series celebrates the huge contribution
that Britain's black community has made to the
development of contemporary British style.

John Galliano, Autumn/Winter 04/05 collection. In response to demands from friends for clothing that paralleled the flamboyance, drama and superb cut of his collections for women, John Galliano launched his menswear line. Galliano worked with Tommy Nutter whilst training at Central Saint Martins, and this collection combines extremely sharp tailoring with the bias cut that made Galliano's name during his early days as creative director at the Parisian house of Givenchy.

pictures reposition what Evans describes as the 'missing cultures of urban Britain' in the popular consciousness. Foxton's styling made the link between the two cultures' tailoring and sartorial traditions, the austerity, restraint, colour and volume of the 'click' suit directly referencing the ascetic modernism of Brummellian dandyism (opposite). As Evans points out, 'Dandyism is about attitude, not race'.

Attitude remains central to the New Briton. A generation of designers and individuals have returned to an exploration of national stereotypes (be they British or otherwise), bringing to bear multiple cultural signifiers on a shared investment in masculine style. The menswear collection launched in 2004 by John Galliano, a sartorial master of cultural investigation, has been described as a 'flamboyant dressing-up box of *Boy's Own* references'. Galliano says:

It's like a gentlemen's club: on the one side you have a very strict, conservative type and on the other the naughty pin-up – but the overall impact is masculine.

His technical virtuosity is demonstrated in the application of the more feminine bias cut to achingly sharp Savile Row tailoring. He combines a lightness of touch and hidden details. The look is classic, but, as Galliano explains, it feels as though 'you're wearing a tracksuit – mercurial, liquid oil around your body – because the fabrics drape and mould'. A product of multiple cultural influences (his parents are Spanish

and he was brought up in Gibraltar and the UK), Galliano has consistently demonstrated how a pertinent raiding of historical and cultural reference can be deployed as commentary on contemporary society:

Whether it's the influence of our American or Hispanic brothers, taking pride in how you look isn't something to shy away from anymore… the British man today is probably more black or Latin in his sensibility than he's ever been… That mixing of cultures feeds back into clothes.[7]

Interview with Bayode Oduwole

Former scientist and Department of Health employee, Bayode Oduwole is the co-founder of design and retail outlet Pokit in Fernhead Road, Queen's Park, London.

AC: How and why did you get into design?
BayO: By accident…and not by accident: a combination of frustration at what was out there, and my many experiences of London's hybrid culture.
AC: What does Pokit stand for?
BayO: A lot of what Pokit represents is a challenge to established attitudes, but our method is non-confrontational. The twentieth-century punk approach is too literal for us. We offer cool and style with the same fervour for quality of service and design as any of the established brands. In an age where short-term,

Right: John Galliano, Spring/Summer 2005 collection.

Opposite: LCFP (London College of Fashion Presents), Spring/Summer 2003 collection. Chris Choi's graduate collection, entitled 'Nostalzia', was immediately acquired by the Victoria & Albert Museum, which provided the backdrop for the collection shown here (see p. 150). The 2003 collection, entitled 'Dark Summer in London', explored stereotypical portrayals of British masculinity found in the East End, from the immigrant to the rock star and from Jack the Ripper to the doctor.

lifestyle branding dominates the market, Pokit offers innovation, substance and quality. Design is a question and answer vehicle; aesthetics and function are the same thing. Pokit is a modern outfitter without the nostalgic hangover.

AC: Is cultural influence important in what you do?

BayO: No, because good design is good design whatever its origins. Yes, because I live in a world where influences, information and images from wide sources are more accessible than ever. Pokit's stylistic references are culturally eclectic, ranging from the Wild West to Nigeria, from Nottingham to Morocco; what we're interested in is educating people about the history of a style rather than providing people with decorative ethnicity. New Briton is, for us, British style at its best, as it has always been, the simultaneous cultural regard and disregard is old and new. Curry is the national dish, tea is not grown in the UK but is a national pastime, crockery is called china, sugar comes from the Indies in boxes marked Tate & Lyle. This, combined with dissent and experimentation, is the benevolent paradox entrenched in the fabric of the British psyche.

AC: You have specifically chosen a retail space off the beaten track, in west London. What drove that choice?

BayO: 'Real' London has always had authenticity. Fashion has become so dumbed-down, all about one main trend, that a shop in a less conspicuous area now seems so much more startling.

AC: Is there anything dandy in what you do?

BayO: Dandy has become so generic and misused as a term, so I'll start by saying I'm no fop or *macaroni*[8]. Pokit is a modern, international, English-based design company, understated and sartorially correct. Our clothes are traditional without being wistful; our style is quite 'proper' – brown shoes should not be worn after 6pm – but the focus is on function. If that sums up dandy in the original sense, then yes there is much that is dandy in what we do. There's a totality to the Pokit look, but also an ambiguity that could certainly be read as dandy. Pokit pieces are expensive, but they offer real value. They are well-designed, well-made, familiarly unfamiliar items. Somewhere in that mix comes distinction.

Interview with Robin Dutt

Robin Dutt is one of London's most famed dandies, a journalist and an author. When not writing, he spends most of his days at Home House, a private club, in London's Portman Square.

AC: What do you understand dandyism to be?

RD: Dandyism is the last vestige of a sartorial spirituality. It is also the last port in an antique world, which is hardly ever visited by vessels of new hope. But should a passing ship dock there, or even be shipwrecked close by, a certain elegant salvation is close at hand. Dandyism is purposefully a place of solitude, isolation and contemplation. It is a secular

monastery but with essential accessories.

AC: If you had to describe dandyism in a sound bite...

RD: A dandy teaches something that few will learn – by example alone.

AC: The current debate around dandyism has proposed that it's no longer possible to be anything but a sartorial replica of Brummell's original dandy, that to live the lifestyle and philosophy is impossible in the twenty-first century. Would you agree or disagree?

RD: To be a sartorial replica of The Beau is totally impossible and wholly undesirable. Those who state the contrary have not the slightest notion of his role and import as a man and as a force. One cannot imitate him. And, as the old saying goes, those who attempt to do so end up looking more like the Prince Regent. However, it is entirely possible to eschew as far as possible the main vulgarities of the contemporary movement with all its emphasis on speed, performance and celebrity, and peruse such things as grace, charm, politeness, dignity and strength of character. A feeling for fair play, a sense of worth but not self-aggrandisement and a definite conception of one's ultimate 'apartness' from the society in which one happens to be – this time around.

AC: How important is the lifestyle and philosophy?

RD: Dandyism is its own lifestyle and philosophy. It does not need vast tomes written about it. Nothing can be gleaned from an exhaustive 'style post-mortem'. One simply is or is not a dandy. One knows it. And, one knows pretenders to its attic crown. But if there had to be a lifestyle and philosophy of dandyism, one might say that it centres on the very core of the dandy's existence, on his raison d'être, on his sense of being in the world and, of course, on his sense of being at the centre of his own unpopulated universe.

AC: My understanding of your practice is that you are a dandy in the fullest sense. Please describe why and how this practice manifests itself in your daily life.

RD: In the first instance, one does not plan to have a 'dandy day' per se. The most crucial thing is that although one breathes the same air (although necessarily filtered by the dandy nose) and shares walking space and travelling space with the world, the dandy must be aware of himself at all times. How he holds himself, behaves, thinks, dreams. As a one-time dandy-esque creature, Sir Hardy Amies wrote a man should choose his clothes well, put them on carefully and then forget all about them – or words to that effect. The man he spoke of was not a run-of-the-mill human being, nor yet perhaps a dandy. But the phrase certainly betrays a dandy's sense of appearance, which whilst being exquisite is not obvious and actually can look on occasions a little deliciously *dégagé*. Studied negligence, *peut-être*?

AC: What is it about dandyism that attracted you?

RD: Dandyism chose me. You cannot choose it.

AC: There are a few dedicated people who wear only eighteenth-century clothing and who would no doubt call themselves dandies. My reading is that the modernist in Brummell would have considered this in direct opposition to his own very modern sensibilities.

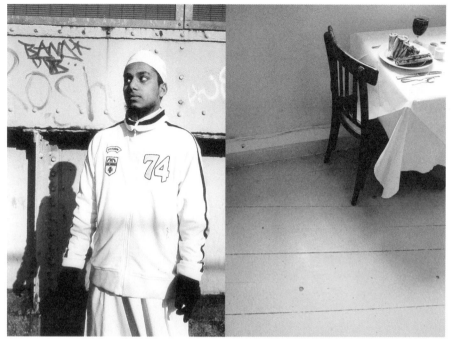

Right: Bangladeshi boy (2003). This image was shot for the British Council's touring exhibition '21st Century Dandy' and shows a young boy combining national dress with more traditional markers of British street culture (a football top and expensive trainers).

Far right: St John restaurant, Smithfields. Opened in 1994 by chef Fergus Henderson and business partner Trevor Gulliver, St John is famed for its contemporary exploration of traditional British food. It is located in an old smokehouse directly opposite Smithfields meat market.

RD: Brummell represented the new in so many ways. His eighteenth-century late Georgian and early Regency companions dressed in silk fondue fancies in anything from strawberry to teal and were becoming more and more like the memory of the corsages of Madame de Pompadour. Brummell's view was revolutionary. He scented the birth of the new century, helped propel it along through his own edict, appearance, advice and public *bons mots*. By Brummell's sartorial standards, the over-feathered peacocks should have been shot before they could come screeching into a gilded drawing room. His version of sartorial elegance has certainly stood the test of time: dark, masculine-looking, form-fitting, handsome, practical and elegant clothes that say nothing about the tailor of the garment and everything about the wearer.

AC: Your collection includes a number of eighteenth-century pieces, but you combine these with Vivienne Westwood and other contemporary labels. Why?

RD: If one has an eye for detail and marries correct line with correct line, one can mix anything with anything. But only *if*.

AC: The New Briton investigates cultural fusion, the way in which designers have played with archetypes of Englishness, of which the dandy is one. A lot of this is about a blend of aristocratic or traditional clothing with street or working-class style. To me, Brummell's practice was also a re-positioning of working clothing into a totally different context. How do you read this?

RD: Brummell's origins were not aristocratic, but hard-working and money-gathering lower-middle class. There was no pride necessarily about lowly birth, but certainly pride in the fact that through diligence a man could rise and rise and even surpass gilded crowns to be celebrated in history. Brummell's 'honesty' in terms of his selection of plain wools, highly starched cottons and fine linen, and his reduction of colour and volume to the now recognizably masculine tones of dark blue, buff and yellow, or midnight blue-black for tail-coats, hint at the uniformed male population who adopted this style en masse from the middle of Victoria's reign. It does seem democratic, honest, simple, plain, humble even, but we must recall that Brummell suffered no fool gladly, especially tailors. So the story goes that someone once seeking sartorial opinion from him was trounced with 'D'ye call that *thing* a coat?' Cruel, but probably true.

AC: You've been a dandy all your life. Would you agree that there seems to be a renaissance in this practice, or is it just a flourishing of typically English sartorial rebellion in the face of global fashion homogeneity?

RD: Fashion is cyclical. It always will be. The fact that fashion features dandy items is of no import. Dandyism is not a trend, it is a *raison d'être*, a wonderful prison you can never escape from and to which no reprieve will be sent.

Mahmoud,
designer, on the
deck, Tattershall
Castle, London.

Arkadius, designer, in his store, Porchester Place, London.

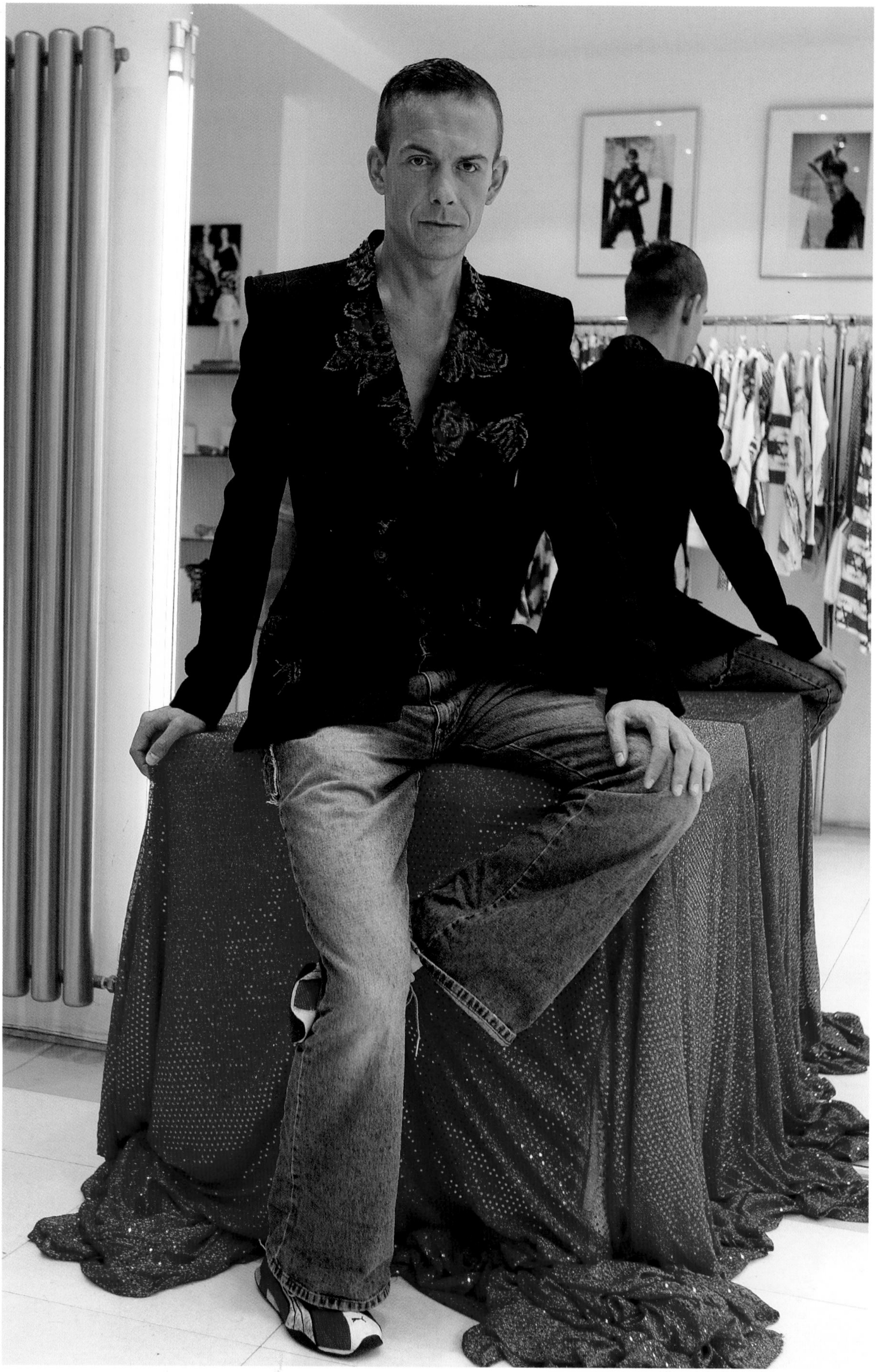

Bayode Oduwole,
designer, in his
store, Fernhead
Road, London.

Danny di Massa, on the stairs of his tattoo studio, Frith Street, London.

Diasuke, designer, at the skate park, Brixton, London.

Chris Choi,
designer, in
Portman Square,
London.

Andreas
Kronthaler,
design director
at Vivienne
Westwood,
at the florist,
Wandsworth.

Mehbs Yaquib,
designer, at
Sketch, Conduit
Street, London.

Robin Dutt, writer, at his club, Home House, Portman Square, London.

Stephen Jones,
milliner, in Soho
Square, London.

Walé Adayemi, designer, outside his studio, Links Yard, London.

Simon Fraser, jeweller and course director at Central Saint Martins, at work, Southampton Row, London.

Peter Jensen,
designer, in his
studio,
Shacklewell Lane,
London.

Alan Kennedy,
stylist and
fashion
consultant,
Heddon Street,
London.

Details of the gentlemen's grooming establishment,
Geo F. Trumper, Curzon Street, London.

Notes

Introduction

1 'Strictly the term [Regency] should be reserved for the styles current between 1811 when George Prince of Wales became Regent and 1820 when he succeeded as George IV (or 1830 when he died), but these dates are without artistic significance. The term Regency provides, however, a useful label for the predominant style in England from the 1790s until the early Victorian 1940s.' Fleming, John and Hugh Honour, The Penguin Dictionary of Decorative Arts, Penguin, London, 1979, p. 648.

2 Moers, Ellen, *The Dandy: Brummell to Beerbohm*, Secker & Warburg, London, 1960, pp 31–33.

3 Bulwer-Lytton, Edward, *Pelham; Or, the Adventures of a Gentleman*, Leipzig, London, 1834, pp 180–82.

4 Barbey D'Aurevilly, Jules, 'Du Dandysme et de Georges Brummell', trans. George Walden, *Who Is A Dandy?*, Gibson Square Books, London, 2002, pp 78–79.

5 Moers, Ellen, *The Dandy: Brummell to Beerbohm*, p. 167.

6 Ibid., pp 181–82. *Macaronis* were mid-nineteenth-century, cosmopolitan Londoners, so-called after the Macaroni Club of 1764.

7 Breward, Christopher, 'The Dandy Laid Bare', Stella Bruzzi and Pamela Church-Gibson, *Fashion Cultures: Theories, Explorations and Analysis*, Routledge, London, 2000, p. 222.

8 Ibid., p. 228.

9 Ibid., p. 229.

10 The beginnings of the homosexual rights movement can be traced to 1969 and the (largely gay frequented) Stonewall Bar in New York's lower Manhattan. For the first time on record, homosexual patrons fought back when Stonewall was raided one hot summer night by New York City policemen hoping to arrest gay individuals for engaging in then illegal homosexual acts.

11 Compton, Nick, 'Where now for the straight guy?', *i-D*, 'The After Dark Issue', Levelprint, London, no. 245, July 2004, p. 98.

12 Breward, Christopher, 'The Dandy Laid Bare', p. 230. Breward was writing about late-nineteenth-century dandyism.

13 Eshun, Ekow, 'Content Culture', *Viewpoint*, issue 15, Metropolitan Publishing BV, Amsterdam, 2004, p. 137.

14 Victoria Postrel quoted in, Compton, Nick, 'MassClassPromise', *Viewpoint*, issue 15, Metropolitan Publishing BV, Amsterdam, 2004, p. 51.

15 Walden, George, *Who Is a Dandy?*, Gibson Square Books, London, 2002, p. 57.

16 Breward, Christopher, 'The Dandy Laid Bare', p. 231.

17 Thomas Carlyle's sardonic dismissal of the dandy in *Sartor Resartus*, written in the 1830s.

18 Moers, Ellen, *The Dandy: Brummell to Beerbohm*, p. 318.

The Gentleman

1 It is no coincidence that the Regency dandy adopted the clothing of England's landed gentry, although it was Thomas, Coke of Norfolk who first wore this sombre dress, riding boots and top hat to the Court, about fifty years before the rise of Brummell. 'Brummell saw instinctively that the day of aristocracy was over and that the day of gentility had arrived.'

2 Mason, Philip, *The English Gentleman: The Rise and Fall of an Ideal*, William Morrow & Co, New York, 1982, p. 93.

3 Wilson, Elizabeth, *Adorned in Dreams*, Virago Press, London, 1985, p. 173.

Neo-Modernist

1 Breward, Christopher, 'The Dandy Laid Bare', Stella Bruzzi and Pamela Church-Gibson, *Fashion Cultures: Theories, Explorations and Analysis*, Routledge, London, 2000, p. 234.

2 Baudelaire, Charles, 'The Painter of Modern Life', trans. PE Charvet, *Baudelaire: Selected Writings on Art and Artists*, Cambridge University Press, Cambridge, 1972, p. 420.

3 Wigley, Mark, 'White Out: Fashioning the Modern', ed. D Fausch, *Architecture: In Fashion*, Princeton Architectural Press, New York, 1996, p. 154.

4 Polhemus, Ted, *Streetstyle*, Thames & Hudson, London, 1994, p. 19.

5 Ibid., p. 20.

6 Ibid., p. 51.

7   MacInnes, Colin, *Absolute Beginners*, Allison & Busby, London, 1992, p. 62.

8   Hebdige, Dick, 'The Meaning of Mod, eds. Stuart Hall and Tony Jefferson, *Resistance Through Rituals: Youth subcultures in post-war Britain*, Routledge, London, 1993 [first published CCCS, Birmingham, 1979], p. 93.

9   Cicolini, Alice, *21st Century Dandy*, British Council, London, 2002.

10 Alexander McQueen press release for the launch of his menswear collection.

East End Flâneur

1   Bolton, Andrew, *The Supermodern Wardrobe*, Victoria & Albert Publications, London, 2002, p. 7.

2   Halévy, Daniel, quoted in Walter Benjamin, *The Arcades Project*, ed. Roy Tiedemann, trans. Howard Eiland and Kevin McLaughlin, Harvard University Press, Boston, 2003, p. 444.

3   Foucault, Michel, quoted in Caroline Evans 'The Enchanted Spectacle' *Fashion Theory*, Berg Publishers, Oxford, vol. 5, issue 3, August 2001, p. 306.

4   Bracewell, Michael, 'Gilbert & George: True Pioneers of East End Art', *The Telegraph*, Telegraph Group, London, 31 March 2004, telegraph.co.uk.

5   Wilson, Elizabeth, *Bohemians: The Glamorous Outcasts*, I.B. Tauris, London, 2000. p. 24.

6   The East End has 'the highest concentration of artists in Europe' according to www.whitecube.com.

7   Wilson, Elizabeth *Bohemians: The Glamorous Outcasts*, p. 165.

Celebrity Tailor

1   Although it was James Poole who launched the business in 1806, it was his son, Henry, who shot to fame and fortune on taking over in 1846.

2   Tommy Nutter quoted in O'Neill, Alistair, *Tommy Nutter and the Disproportionate Suit*, (unpublished) a lecture for London College of Fashion, 2002.

3   Ibid.

4   Breward, Christopher, 'In Conversation with Richard James', unpublished.

Terrace Casual

1   Polhemus, Ted, *Streetstyle*, Thames & Hudson, London, 1994, p. 100.

2   Breward, Christopher, 'The Dandy Laid Bare', Stella Bruzzi and Pamela Church-Gibson, *Fashion Cultures: Theories, Explorations and Analysis*, Routledge, London, 2000, p. 225.

3   Cicolini, Alice, *21st Century Dandy*, British Council, London, 2002.

4   *Quincy* was a late 1970s to mid-1980s American daytime TV show, featuring a lead character of the same name.

New Briton

1   Cicolini, Alice, *21st Century Dandy*, British Council, London, 2002.

2   John Galliano, quoted in 'Gentlemen, Please Be Upstanding', *i-D*, Levelprint, London, July 2004, pp 94–95.

3   Dalrymple, William *White Mughals*, HarperCollins, London, 2002, p. xli.

4   Davey, Kevin, *English Imaginaries: Anglo-British Approaches to Modernity*, Lawrence & Wishart, London, 1999, p. 2.

5   Ibid., p. 115.

6   Ibid., p. 127.

7   John Galliano, quoted in 'Gentlemen, Please Be Upstanding', pp 94–95.

8   *See* Introduction, note 6.

Bibliography

Baudelaire, Charles
Baudelaire: Selected Writings on Art and Artists,
trans. PE Charvet, Cambridge University Press,
Cambridge, 1972.

Benjamin, Walter
The Arcades Project, ed. Roy Tiedemann, trans.
Howard Eiland and Kevin McLaughlin, Harvard
University Press, Boston, 2003.

*Charles Baudelaire: A Lyric Poet in the Era of
High Capitalism*, trans. H. Zohn, New Left Books,
London, 1973.

Bennett-England, Rodney
Dress Optional: A Revolution in Menswear, Peter Owen,
London, 1967.

Bourdieu, Pierre
*Distinction: A Social Critique of the Judgement of
Taste*, Routledge & Kegan Paul Ltd., London, 1984.

Breward Christopher
'The Dandy Laid Bare', Stella Bruzzi and Pamela
Church-Gibson, *Fashion Cultures: Theories,
Explorations and Analysis*, Routledge, London, 2000.

'Twenty First Century Dandy: The Legacy of Beau
Brummell' *21st Century Dandy*, British Council,
London, 2002.

Breward, Christopher, Becky Conekin and Caroline Cox, eds.
The Englishness of English Dress, Berg Publishers,
Oxford, 2002.

Bruzzi, Stella and Pamela Church-Gibson
Fashion Cultures: Theories, Explorations and Analysis,
Routledge, London, 2000.

Cohn, Nik
*Today there are no Gentlemen: The changes in
Englishmen's Clothes Since the War*, Weidenfeld and
Nicolson, London, 1971.

Cole, Shaun
Don We Now Our Gay Apparel, Berg Publishers, Oxford,
2000.

Conrad, Peter
'Beaton in Brilliantia', Terence Pepper, *Beaton
Portraits*, National Portrait Gallery, London, 2004.

Cook, Pam
*Fashioning the Nation: Costume and Identity in British
Cinema*, BFI Publishing, London, 1996.

Cruise, Colin
'19th Century Artists Clothes', *The Gendered Object*,
ed. Pat Kirkham, Manchester University Press,
Manchester, 1996.

Davey, Kevin
*English Imaginaries: Anglo-British Approaches to
Modernity*, Lawrence & Wishart, London, 1999.

Dyer, Richard
Stars, BFI Publishing, London, 1998.

Ewen, Stuart
*All Consuming Images: The Politics of Style in
Contemporary Culture*, Basic Books, New York, 1988.

Evans, Caroline & Thornton, Mina
Women in Fashion, Quartet, London, 1989.

Fillin-Yeh, Susan, ed
Dandies: Fashion and Finesse in Art and Culture, New
York University Press, New York, 2001.

Flusser, Alan
*Dressing the Man: Mastering the Art of Permanent
Fashion*, HarperCollins, New York, 2002.

Foulkes, Nick
*Last of the Dandies: The Scandalous Life and Escapades
of Count D'Orsay*, Little Brown and Company, London,
2003.

Green, Jonathon
  All Dressed Up: The Sixties and the Counterculture, Pimlico, London, 1999.

Hall, Stuart and Tony Jefferson
  Resistance Through Rituals: Youth Subcultures in Post-War Britain, HarperCollins, London, 1991 [first published Centre for Contemporary Cultural Studies, Birmingham, 1979].

Harper, Sue
  Picturing the Past: The Rise and Fall of the British Costume Film, BFI Publishing, London, 1994.

Harvey, John
  Men in Black, Reaktion Books, London, 1995.

Hebdige, Dick
  Subculture: The Meaning of Style, London: Routledge, 2003 [first published Methuen, London, 1979].

Kaplan, Joel H and Sheila Stowell
  Theatre & Fashion: Oscar Wilde to the Suffragettes Cambridge University Press, Cambridge, 1995.

Kureishi, Hanif and Jon Savage, eds
  The Faber Book of Pop, Faber and Faber, London, 1995.

Laver, James
  Dandies, Weidenfeld and Nicolson, London, 1968.

Mason, Philip
  The English Gentleman: The Rise and Fall of an Ideal, William Morrow & Co, New York, 1982.

Melly, George
  Revolt into Style: The Pop Arts in Britain, Penguin, London, 1972.

Moers, Ellen
  The Dandy: Brummell to Beerbohm, Secker & Warburg, London, 1960, pp 31–33.

Mort, Frank
  Cultures of Consumption: Masculinities and Social Space in Late Twentieth-Century Britain, Routledge, London, 1996

Mulvagh, Jane
  Vivienne Westwood: An Unfashionable Life, HarperCollins, London, 1998.

Polhemus, Ted
  Streetstyle, Thames & Hudson, London, 1994.

Temple, Gustav and Vic Darkwood
  The Chap Manifesto: Revolutionary Etiquette for the Modern Gentleman, Fourth Estate, London, 2001.

Tomlinson, Alan
  'Sport, Leisure & Style', *British Cultural Studies: Geography, Nationality and Identity*, eds David Morley and Kevin Robins, Oxford University Press, Oxford, 2001.

Walden, George
  Who Is a Dandy?, Gibson Square Books, London, 2002.

Wilson, Elizabeth
  Adorned in Dreams, Virago Press, London, 1985.

  Bohemians: The Glamorous Outcasts, I.B. Tauris, London, 2000.

Woollen, Peter
  Raiding the Icebox: Reflections on Twentieth-Century Culture, Verso, London, 1993.

York, Peter
  Style Wars, Sidgwick & Jackson, London, 1980.

Tailor's Glossary

Back pleat: Pleat-fronted trousers usually have two sets of pleats. Back pleats are located between the front pleats and the side seams.

Back vent: The slit at the back of a jacket, which varies in length depending on the style.

Bal collar: The name refers to Balmacaan, an old estate in Inverness, Scotland. A high collar, 3 or 4 inches wide, it is worn flat against the chest or turned up and buttoned across with a strip of fabric stitched on the collar's underside.

Barrel cuff: A shirt cuff made from a single layer of fabric and fastened with a button (not cuff links).

Basting: Loose temporary stitches on a garment assembled for first fitting.

Besom: An insert pocket made with a narrow welted (or jetted) edge above the pocket opening. A double besom pocket has welts on both the top and bottom edges and a flapped besom has a flap added.

Bush jacket: A single-breasted shirt jacket, belted, with four flapped patch pockets, usually made in cotton drill or gabardine in a tan or beige colour.

Button stance: The positioning of buttons, determined by their relationship to a jacket's front edge and waist.

Canvases: An internal canvas is used to mould the fabric of a suit jacket to a client's body shape. Canvases are made from linen, horsehair, hemp, jute and other heavy materials. The kind of material used for a canvas depends entirely on the weight of the fabric used for the garment.

Chalk stripe: Mirroring the line of the tailor's chalk, this stripe is woven in a rope-like effect on the material.

Coatmaker: There are specialist tailors not only for types of garment (trousers, smoking jackets), but also for parts that comprise the garment (sleeves, canvases). In this case, the term refers to the maker of jackets.

Cork: Tailoring slang for The Boss or manager of the cutting room.

'D' pocket tack: The mark of highest quality bespoke, this invisible tack is stitched, in a D-shape, from seam to seam on a jetted pocket to reinforce the seams' ends and to prevent them coming undone.

Doctor: Tailoring slang for an alteration tailor. Alterations are carried out by highly specialized tailors trained to make fine changes to the fit of garments that are required in the late stages of the process.

English back: Trousers cut in this style curve up at the back to a peak where suspenders are attached.

Forward pleat: Trousers cut with pleats facing forwards towards the fly rather than away from it; this style is usually associated with English tailoring.

Finisher: Hand-sewn finishing is one of the telltale signs of bespoke tailoring; buttonholes and the securing of the lining and stitching to the edges of the garment are carried out by hand. It is also the final part of the process and does not take place until all the alterations have been made.

French cuff: A dress-shirt cuff, double in length and turned back, with two small buttonholes that fasten with cuff links.

Fusing: The heat-welding of canvas to the fabric. In bespoke it is only ever used for very lightweight fabric.

Gimping: The gimping machine concurrently decorates and trims the edges of leather pieces that go to make a shoe's upper. The tool pieces can be changed to provide variations in pattern.

Gorge: The place where collar and label meet. In Savile Row tailoring, this indent appears high on the chest.

Gun flap: Although it is a decorative feature today, the extra flap of fabric on a hunting jacket originally gave the wearer added protection against the impact of a shotgun's recoil.

Jetted pocket: An inset pocket finished around the edge with binding or piping, usually without a flap. A moon-jetted pocket takes the shape of a crescent moon (downturned) and is a speciality of John Pearse.

Jigger button: The tailor's name for the small, additional button on the inside of a double-breasted coat that prevents the inside flap from dropping below the hem of the front piece.

Kill: Tailoring slang for a spoiled job.

Kipper: Tailoring slang for a female tailor. It stems from the fact that most female tailors wanted to work in pairs to avoid unwelcome advances. It is also slang for the wide tie brought to fashionable prominence in the 1960s by shirtmaker Michael Fish.

Made to: Short for 'made to measure', a process whereby an existing block is altered to fit a client. Far less detailed than bespoke, made to only allows a few adjustments. The bespoke garment is built up entirely from scratch to suit the customer.

Monk-strap shoe: A plain-toed shoe with a buckle strap over the arch.

Piece work: Most Savile Row tailors are self-employed and paid a fixed rate per garment (determined by the garment's complexity), known as the piece rate.

Pig: Tailoring slang for an unclaimed garment.

Pork: Tailoring slang for a misfit rejected by a customer, but which might be sold elsewhere.

Reverse pleat: The opposite of a forward pleat, the reverse pleat faces backwards towards the pockets, creating a flatter shape.

Scye: A tailor will take several measurements to perfect the scye, or armhole, as correct fit is crucial to prevent the back of the jacket rising up when seated. Being so fitted, it is often very noticeable to first-time bespoke clients.

Sham buttonhole: A false buttonhole.

Shawl collar: Also know as a roll lapel, it is a combined lapel and collar; the under collar is cut in one with the garment front and a centre-back seam joins the two halves of the top collar. Most commonly used for dinner jackets.

Short-back balance: A lack of length over the shoulder at the back of a jacket can cause the collar to lift away from the neck or the coat to hang away from the seat.

Short-front balance: A lack of length in the front of a jacket can make it pull away from the body, appearing shorter at the front and stretching open the back vent.

Skiffle: Tailoring slang for a job needed in a hurry.

Slash pocket: Set in between the jacket or coat fabric and its lining, a slash pocket appears vertically or diagonally and is suitable for putting hands in.

Sleeve pitch: The pitch is the angle at which the sleeve is attached to the jacket armhole. It should respond to the arm's angle as it hangs naturally from the shoulder.

Tab: Tailoring slang for particularly difficult customers.

Trimmings: All the materials that go into the making of the suit.

Trotter: Tailoring slang for a messenger or runner of errands.

Tweed merchant: Tailoring slang for a tailor whose role is particularly easy or whose quality of work is poor.

Vicuna: The 'Rolls Royce of wool fibres', as described by Flusser, Vicuna comes from an animal of the same name, similar to the llama and found in the remote Andes. The wool is naturally tobacco coloured.

Welt: A raised or strengthened seam.

Wicking: Natural fibres allow the body to breathe by transferring moisture from the inside of the fabric to its surface, where it evaporates. This process is termed wicking.

Zoot suit: A full-legged man's suit with accompanying long coat. The trousers (32'' at the knee and only 15'' at the bottom) were cuffed and the coat was cut with wide lapels, tapered waist and padded shoulders. It is linked to early 1930s East Coast American jazz culture. The huge quantity of fabric used in its construction meant the suit was banned in 1942 by the War Production Board.

Knitted Tie

Plus-Fours

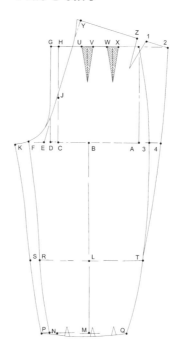

Knitted Tie

The tie is worked in a flat piece on two needles and is then sewn up the long edge to form a circular tie.

Materials:
1 ball (50g) of Clark's Anchor Stranded Cotton and a pair of No. 14 steel knitting needles make a double tie 2 inches wide.

Abbreviations:
K = knit, P = purl, tog = together, M = make.

Cast on 43 stitches and do 3 rows of plain knitting, working into the back of stitches on first row.
4th row: K 3, P 4, * K 2, P 4, repeat from * to end.
5th row: K 3, * M 1 (by bringing the thread to the front of the needle for an open stitch), K 2 tog, K 4, repeat from * until 4 remain, M 1, K 2 tog, K 2.
Repeat the 4th and 5th rows 3 times more, then work the 4th row.
13th, 14th and 15th rows: Plain knitting.
16th row: P 4, * K 2, P 4, repeat from * until 3 remain, K 3.
17th row: K 6, * M 1, K 2 tog, K 4, repeat from *, finishing with K 1.
Repeat the 16th and 17th rows 3 times more, then work the 16th row. This completes one pattern.

Repeat the pattern 7 times more for the long end. Work the first 12 rows of the next pattern.
NEXT row: (K 3, K 2 tog,) 3 times, K 13, (K 2 tog, K 3) 3 times (37 stitches)
Work the 2nd row, and continue pattern up to and including the 12th row.
NEXT row: (K 4, K 2 tog) 6 times, K 1. You have 31 stitches. K 2 rows and P 1 row.
NEXT row: (K 2 tog, K 2) 7 times, K 2 tog, K 1.
There are now 23 stitches, on which P 1 row and K 1 row alternately for 13 sets of ½ inches, finishing with a P row.
NEXT row: (K 1 into front and 1 into back of same stitch, K 2) 7 times, K 1 into front and 1 into back, K 1 (31 stitches).
P 1 row and K 2 rows.
NEXT row: (K 4, K 1 into front, and 1 into back of next stitch) 6 times, K 1, giving 37 stitches in the row.
Begin pattern with 4th row and work up to and including 14th row.
NEXT row: (K 3, K 1 into front, and 1 into back of next stitch) 3 times, K 13 (K 1 into front, and 1 into back of next stitch, K 3) 3 times.
Continue pattern from 4th row then work 4 repeats of pattern and one more repeat to the end of 15th row. K one plain row and cast off.
Press well on wrong side and sew together the long edges for back of tie with sewing silk of the same shade. Press seam to flatten.

Bow Tie

Tying a bow tie, step by step.

Plus-Fours

Measures (in inches):
42 side, 30 leg, 30 waist, 36 seat, knee 23.

Draw line O A 1½, and square from A.
A to B (please note) is one-third scale less ½ inch.
A to C half scale.
C to F one-sixth scale plus ½ inch.
Square up from C to H and from H to O.
Add 1 inch at D and G and draw fly-line.
H to U 2½ inches.
U to V 1½ inches.
V to W 1¾ inches.
W to X 1½ inches.
Square down from B, and make B to L half leg less
2 inches.
L to M 8 inches (more or less according to overlap).
L to T and L to R are one fourth knee; if there is any
difficulty in getting a run, add a little at T.
M to Q and M to N are about 1¼ inches less than at knee.
Add 1 inch from A to 3, and a little round at bottom.
For the undersides, make F to K 1¾ inches, R to S 1
inch, and N to P 1 inch.
From C mark up to J one-fourth scale plus ½ inch,

Point E is midway between C and F.
Rule a line from E through J.
Measure up waist, adding sufficient for seams and
pleats, and a cut in underside and locate 2.
Rest square against seat line and draw from Y to 2.
2 to 1 is 2½ inches; add 1 to 1½ inches from 3 to 4 and
complete.

Guidelines for Bespoke

Recommended reading for a comprehensive guide to colour, proportion, fit and fabric is Alan Flusser's *Dressing the Man* (see p. 164). Although Flusser takes a more transatlantic view of sartorial flair, his knowledge of British tailoring traditions is comprehensive. Nick Foulkes's erstwhile columns for the London *Evening Standard's ES Magazine* are an excellent, highly personalized account of the finer details of masculine dress and grooming for anyone prepared to make the long journey to the British Library's newspaper archives in London's Colindale.

Ordering a suit

Most tailors will outline the required contents of a basic bespoke wardrobe for first-time customers. Terry Haste, managing director of Huntsman & Co, Savile Row, suggests the following for aspiring gentlemen: ten daywear suits, to include one single-breasted, one-button suit in charcoal-grey worsted wool, one stripe and one plaid; three sports jackets, one single-breasted, one-button jacket in tweed and complementary trousers, to include grey flannel and whipcord; one dress overcoat; two day overcoats, one single-breasted, the other double-breasted; two evening wear suits and one evening tails; and one mourning suit.

A tailor also considers a major function of his role to prevent the customer from making expensive misjudgments over fabric and shape. Choosing the shape, colour and fabric of a bespoke suit requires a readiness to look at yourself with some degree of detachment. Colour selection should be made on the basis of complexion and contrast. Flusser makes the point that those with strong contrast (olive skin and light hair or dark hair and light skin) are able to wear starkly opposing colours, whereas those with more tonal complexions (light hair and light skin or dark hair and olive skin) should choose fabrics that are more muted and draw attention to the warmer tints in the face.

Body shape, or what Flusser describes as 'personal architecture', is a mostly unalterable factor in bespoke.

The width of the jacket shoulder is dependent on the width of the head; narrow shoulders work well with a thin face and narrow frame, while wide-cut shoulders suit a wider face and more athletic physique. Jackets should be long enough to cover one's bottom, but should also give as much length as possible to the leg, a particularly delicate balance for shorter, rounder men. (A rough guide to finding the correct jacket length is to halve the distance between the collar seam and the floor.) The placement of buttons is also crucial, with the waist button, the dividing point for the leg and torso, always positioned at $\frac{1}{2}$'' below the natural waist. Dropped lapels flatter a taller, broader man, whilst shorter men should cut their lapels higher up the frame. The single-breasted lapel should cover between two-fifths and three-fifths of the distance between the jacket's chest and shoulder line. Trousers should always complement the cut of the jacket, acting as an extension of the line, and should hang from the waist not the hips. Cuffed trousers should be $1\frac{5}{8}$'' wide and tend to look better on taller men. Plain, seamed trousers should drop slightly to the back of the shoe. All trousers should be wide enough to cover the shoelace.

The British cut is a waisted jacket (giving a slight hourglass effect), with built-up chest, narrow shoulders, high armholes and subtly flared 'skirt' (the section beneath the waist). The jacket has deep side vents, four-button trimmed sleeves (the buttonholes should open) and narrow, tapering trousers. Two-button, single-breasted jackets are more common than the more striking one-button that is a Huntsman signature. It is a style that looks best on tall, slim men, although the fabric, a softer shoulder, a rolled lapel and a pared-down chest can adapt it for less svelte consumers (something that Charlie Allen accomplishes with particular aplomb).

Basic suit cuts are single-breasted with two or three buttons; single-breasted with peaked lapel; double-breasted with either six on two, or four buttons with an extended lapel. Pockets are flapped, jetted or patched; the first two styles should ideally be finished with a hand-sewn welt detail on top and bottom. Angled pockets are common for riding jackets, although the British sometimes transfer the style to daywear suits.

Trousers are either flat-fronted and narrow, with waist adjusters, or are cut fuller with one or two pleats.

The basic suiting fabrics are divided into plain (charcoal-grey and navy Super 100 worsted wools, grey flannel, cashmere and linen), patterned (herringbone; chalk-, pin-, bead- or pearl-stripe; sharkskin; pick-and-pick; bird's eye; nailhead; glen-, Glenurquhart- or Prince of Wales plaid; windowpane-, shepherd's-, puppy- or houndstooth check; and numerous tweeds) or textured (gabardine, silk Dupioni and mohair).

Overcoats include the Crombie, in heavyweight wool; the Chesterfield, a single- or double-breasted coat with angled pockets, usually in grey herringbone; the British Warm, modelled on the military coat, in Melton wool, cavalry twill or cashmere; and the Covert coat, similar in style to the Chesterfield but slimmer and shorter with textured seaming at the cuff and hem.

'Odd' jackets, trousers and blazers have traditionally afforded greater opportunities for personal detailing, although still within established style guidelines. In mid-1920s America, the Brooks Brothers gabardine jacket – with a stitched-in waistband and four pleats either side of the band – was a classic staple, as was the shirred back jacket. The shirred back was originally produced in gabardine, but linen and bold patterned Shetland wool and tweed were introduced as alternative materials. The jacket back is gathered in between the yoke and stitched-in belt. In England, hacking jackets, derived from the traditional riding jacket, have always proved popular 'odd' jackets, giving extra length and are identifiable by the slanted pockets. Popularized in the 1930s and inspired by colonial military tailoring, the safari jacket has a yoke back and front, four gusseted pockets, belt, long sleeves and cuffs and is traditionally made in linen or gabardine. The traditional plain-back blazer style is descended from both the sporting jacket, in serge or brightly striped flannel, and the naval reefer jacket, either single- or double-breasted with gilt buttons. Although it is possible to experiment with colour, the most formal is a solid navy blue.

'Odd' trousers fall into two categories: the wide, full-cut, pleat-fronted trouser with cuffed bottom and creased back and front and a narrow 17.5'' leg (descended from the Oxford bag, characterized by its pleated waistline, baggy knees and bottoms measuring between 22 and 26 inches); or the narrow, flat-fronted trouser, with waist adjusters or back strap, which is worn lower on the hip and generally considered a more elegant and classically English style that works far better with the waisted jacket line. Appropriate fabrics include a lightweight tweed; charcoal flannel, developed by English mills as a serviceable blend of black, white and grey wool and considered the 'blue blazer of odd dress slacks'; wool gabardine, in a lighter grey or tan; wool covert or twill; Glenurquhart plaid; and Bedford cord, in baby or wide-whale.

Kilgour's Hugh Holland outlines the perfect English bespoke wardrobe on the company's website, www.8savilerow.com, and reproduced here:

Heavyweight suits

Material: 100% pure wool worsted, and flannels.
Weight: 13 oz to 16 oz.
Purpose: Freezing days in London, New York and Moscow. Useful for cold-blooded businessmen.
Design: Pinstripe (blue and grey ground), charcoal-grey flannel, plain navy.
Style: Two double-breasted (button 2, show 6) and two single-breasted (button 2).
Features: Excellent crease resistance, makes up beautifully, longevity.
Quantity: Ideally plan to have four suits at this weight.

Medium-weight suits

Material: Pure wool worsted (cloth this weight drapes beautifully when cut in the English style).
Weight: 10 oz to 12 oz.
Purpose: The perfect utility suit ideal for temperatures between 50 and 60 Fahrenheit and use in all environments from the office (standard materials) to the Opera (luxury fibres).
Features: Luxurious fabrics in a huge range of designs.
Quantity: We advise five suits in standard materials for

business and five in finer materials for smart
occasions. Extra trousers advisable.

Lightweight suits

Weight: 7 oz to 9 oz
Purpose: For warm spring and summer.
Features: Choose lighter coloured fabrics in keeping
     with the season. Beige and vanilla hues are
     particularly popular.
Quantity: Again five suits in standard materials and five
     in finer materials such as silk, mohair and high twist
     fine wool.

Overcoats

Material: wool worsted Crombie overcoating, pure
     cashmere and cashmere/wool mixes.
Weight: 16 oz to 26 oz.
Purpose: For wearing outdoors in cold weather.
Features: Camel, dark grey or navy.
Quantity: Three should be plenty.

Sports jackets and blazers

Material: Millionaire cashmere, silk and cashmere, pure
     silk, wools, tweeds and cheviots.
Purpose: Principally semi-informal, these garments can
     be worn on a huge variety of occasions. Dress-down
     Friday means sports jacket for many office workers.
     Blazers, which by no means have to be navy blue, are
     popular at club functions.
Quantity: No limit!

Trousers

Material: High twist woollens, cottons, flannels, cavalry
     twills and corduroys.
Purpose: Whenever shorts are inappropriate!
Features: We favour plain colours with no limit to
     shade.
Quantity: At least 20 pairs per season.

Dress Wear

Dinner jackets and trousers
     Black barathea (one 10 oz, one 12 oz), midnight blue
     wool worsted.
Dinner jacket
     White wool worsted, worn with black trousers.
     The above can be styled single- or double-breasted,
     with peak, notch or Tautz lapel and a standard or
     shawl collar.
Black silk cummerbund to match silk facing on jacket.
Smoking jacket
     Navy, green or maroon silk velvet to be worn with
     trews.
Morning-coat suit
     Black coat, beige waistcoat and grey and black
     striped trousers.
     Matching grey coat, waistcoat and trousers.
Evening dress tails
     Matching black coat with silk facing and trousers,
     White Marcella waistcoat.
Shooting suits
     Two tweed suits.
     Muted check to avoid frightening the birds.

Ordering a shirt

Shirt collars should be chosen on the basis of face
shape – the smaller the face, the more restrained the
collar – and cuffs should always drop at least 1" below
the jacket sleeve. Collar shapes fall into six basic
categories: the turndown or straight collar; the
cutaway or spread collar; tab and pin collars, which
employ a pin or strip of fabric to hold the collar firmly
in place; the detachable collar; and the soft-roll or
button-down collar (see opposite).
     A well-made bespoke shirt can be identified in
various ways: collar bones, preferably in brass, for turndown and cutaway collars; a split yoke, which allows for
a particular shoulder height; exactly matching patterns
at the seams; French, or raised, seams for seams
particularly subject to stress; single-needle, parallel

Collars

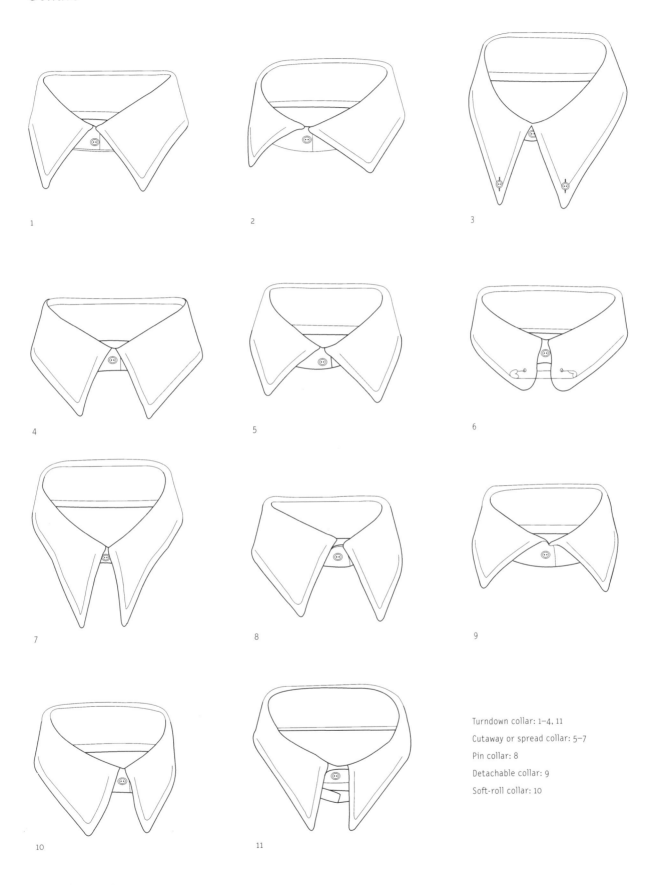

1

2

3

4

5

6

7

8

9

10

11

Turndown collar: 1–4, 11

Cutaway or spread collar: 5–7

Pin collar: 8

Detachable collar: 9

Soft-roll collar: 10

seams, with around twenty stitches per inch, for the remaining seams; a longer-cut back to avoid the shirt lifting out of the trouser waistband; single-button facing with mother-of-pearl buttons; a gusset to reinforce the join of front to back; and multiple pleats at the cuff, with a higher, smaller button to prevent the shirt from gaping.

Good shirting fabrics are cotton or cotton-linen mix, with weights from the dressier broadcloth through the royal Oxford and voile to the standard Oxford cotton. Chambray, poplin and lightweight cotton flannel are also useful, and in the latter case warm, staples. Patterns and colours should be deployed according to complexion contrast, with softer hues and smaller patterns preferable for more muted skin tones. Dominant shirting colours are white and blue, with pink and yellow considered slightly more flamboyant options. Patterns include stripes (Bengal, pencil, hairline, candy, Madras, fancy, shadow, diagonal, bar, track, multi-track and antique track) and checks (fancy, graph, Tattersal, checkerboard, windowpane, pin, hairline and mini-check), but can also be created by the weave itself (Batiste and royal, maize and open-weave Oxford are the standard).

Ordering shoes

A bench-made shoe is characterized by vegetable-tanned, welted soles with hidden stitches (where a strip of leather is stitched in between the edge of the sole and the turned-in upper), up to twelve-week-old skins, leather insoles and linings, and stacked leather heels. Other materials include suede, buckskin and patent and crocodile leather.

In the City, a man wearing brown shoes is considered slightly untrustworthy, so the staple work-wear shoe has traditionally been black despite the fact that darkened antique brown is more complementary to most suiting fabrics. Most styles are based on either a closed- or open-lacing structure. The two sides of the upper and the tongue are stitched under the front section of the shoe in a closed lacing; the tongue is an

extension of the 'vamp', or front, of the shoe and the two sides are stitched on top in an open lacing.

The closed-lacing Oxford style is the classic business shoe, characterized by its stitched toecap, and best worn with wide-legged trousers. The Oxford can be made with slight Brogue detailing across the toecap. The other main closed-lacing style is the Brogue. Similar in shape to the Oxford, it comes in varying degrees of its classic punched and pinked detailing: the full Brogue; the textured half Brogue, where the toecap is fully detailed; and a half Oxford, half Brogue with a strip of punched detailing across the toe cap and around the stitching enclosing the lacing and tongue. In America, the Brogue is known as the Wing-Tip because of its curved toecap, which can sometimes extend all the way around to the back of the shoe.

Open-laced styles again fall into two basic categories – the Derby (or Blucher in America), which has a plain toe; and variations on the Oxford and Brogue that are made with a toecap. Although their open lacing makes these styles less formal, they also tend to be more comfortable as the two side pieces allow for greater adjustment and fit.

Other footwear staples include the dress loafer (which incorporates the American Bass Weejun and Sebago Beefroll, the Italian lightweight leather slip-on and the traditional English tasselled loafer), the Monk-Strap (a plain-toed shoe with a buckle strap over the arch), the Turf or Chukka boot, the Spectator or Correspondent (a two-tone, closed-lace Oxford-Brogue hybrid) and the dress slipper (either in patent leather with grosgrain ribbon or in monogrammed velvet).

Directory

Tailors

Charlie Allen: +44 (0)20 7359 0883
Anderson & Sheppard: www.anderson-sheppard.co.uk
Richard Anderson: www.richardandersonltd.co.uk
Tom Baker: +44 (0)20 7439 9834
Ozwald Boateng: www.ozwaldboateng.com
Timothy Everest: www.timothyeverest.co.uk
Gieves & Hawkes: www.gievesandhawkes.com
Hunstman & Co: www.h-huntsman.com
Richard James: www.richardjames.co.uk
Chris Kerr: www.eddiekerr.co.uk
Kilgour: www.8savilerow.com
Tony Lutwyche: www.lutwyche.co.uk
John Pearse: www.johnpearse.co.uk
Henry Poole & Co: www.henrypoole.com
Mark Powell: www.markpowellbespoke.co.uk
Maurice Sedwell: www.savilerowtailor.com
Dominic Shortle: dominicshortlelondon.com
Spencer Hart: www.spencerhart.com

Designers

Walé Adayemi: info@waleadayemi.co.uk
Arkadius: www.arkadius.com
John Galliano: www.johngalliano.com
Peter Jensen: mail@peterjensenltd.com
Kim Jones: +44 (0)20 7491 3900
Michiko Koshino: www.michikokoshino.com
LCFP: www.lcfplondon.com
Alexander McQueen: www.alexandermcqueen.com
Jonathan Saunders: j.saundersstudio4@btinternet.com
Hannah Small: hrmsmall@hotmail.com
Paul Smith: www.paulsmith.co.uk
Vivienne Westwood: www.viviennewestwood.co.uk

Ready-to-Wear

6876: www.sixeightsevensix.co.uk
Aquascutum: www.aquascutum.co.uk
Belstaff: www.belstaff.com
Brooks Brothers: www.brooksbrothers.com
Burberry and Burberry Prorsum: www.burberry.com
Thomas Burberry: www.thomasburberry.com

Burro: www.burro.co.uk
Cordings: www.cordings.co.uk
Duffer of St. George: www.thedufferofstgeorge.com
Elk: www.oipolloi.com
Griffin: www.griffin-studio.com
Lonsdale: www.lonsdale-sports.com
Lyle & Scott: www.lyleandscott.com
Maharishi: www.emaharishi.com
Oi Polloi: www.oipolloi.com
One True Saxon: www.brownbagclothing.co.uk
Fred Perry: www.fredperry.com
Pokit: www.pokit.co.uk
Pringle of Scotland: www.pringle-of-scotland.co.uk
John Smedley: www.smedley.co.uk
Topman: www.topman.com
Vexed Generation: www.vexed.co.uk

Grooming and Accessories

Ben Day/Isabelle Starling: +44 (0)20 7274 9977
Bill Amberg: www.billamberg.com
Judy Blame: eduardojm@ntlworld.com
George Cox: www.georgecox.co.uk
Crockett & Jones: www.crockettandjones.co.uk
Czech & Speake: www.czechspeake.com
Nicolas Deakins: www.nicolasdeakins.com
Dunhill: www.dunhill.com
Floris: www.florislondon.com
Holland & Holland: www.hollandandholland.com
Stephen Jones: www.stephenjonesmilliner.com
John Lobb: www.johnlobb.com
Lock & Co: www.lockhatters.co.uk
Tanner Krolle: www.tannerkrolle.co.uk
Geo F Trumper: www.trumpers.com
Jeffery West: www.jeffery-west.co.uk

Picture Credits